The Generous Years

The

Generous Years

Remembrances of a frontier boyhood

by Chet Huntley

RANDOM HOUSE   *New York*

To MOTHER and DAD
To WADINE, MARIAN and PEGGY
To TIPPY
To SHARON and LEANNE,
who may now know more about their father
And all in the hope and trust
that GRANDMA and GRANDPA would approve

Contents

The Land

The iron tires of the spring wagon rolled silently along the twin wheel tracks worn into the grass: parallel trails wandering northward and away to their vanishing point on the treeless folds of the benchland. Behind, the rudimentary road dipped and disappeared into the river valley.

As the weight of the wagon eased on their collars, the team of grays, sensing unhitching and feed, blew out their nostrils and swung into an easy, mile-consuming trot, manes flying in the March wind. The muffled thud of the hooves, the occasional creak of the wagon, the jangle of the tug chains and bridle snaps were high-spirited rhythmic beats augmenting the melody . . . the melody of the grass . . . the song of the immense and boundless land.

Sha-a-a-a-a-e-e-e-sha-o-o-o-m-m-m-m.

It rose out of the land, filled it sky to sky; waves of sound, rolling, rolling, building and diminishing. Toward the source of the wind, to the west, the grass sang in shrill sibilance . . . the reed and flute sections. The violins and horns were on the lee side, and their voices were picked up by the wind and carried over the endless sea of grass.

Sha-a-a-a-ae-e-e-e-e-sh-o-o-o-o-o-m-m-m-m-m!

Wind and grass in assonant conversation. The grass
. . . the incredible grass! In March it was only the dried
remains of the last year's growth, which had borne up
and withstood the crushing weight of the winter snow.
Indeed, it had carried the weight of the snow crop like
a forest of supporting beams and pillars. In places the
snow might come only within proximity of the earth,
and as it melted, the drops of water trickled down the
myriad stems and blades. Then the dead stalks, free of
encumbrance, performed their ballet to the wind, before succumbing, as nutrient, to the rush of new
growth surging up from the burgeoning soil.

"Buffalo grass" (*Buchloë dactyloides*), it was called,
and it had been host to the tremendous herds which
had thrived on the broad plateau rolling gently upward
and northward from the Milk River, across the Canadian border, and a hundred miles or so into Alberta,
Saskatchewan and Manitoba. From east to west, the
grass ocean stretched undulating from the base of the
Canadian and Montana Rockies, across North Dakota
and the lower halves of the Canadian provinces to the
fringe of the Minnesota-Manitoba lake country.

From every spring or creek, from every swale and
gully where the snow water collected and remained
through the hot summers, thousands of buffalo trails
radiated out toward the endless pasture land. Millions
of sharp hooves had cut deep paths into the earth and
carved terraces on the hillsides. A hundred years of
domestic grazing, cultivation, and the consequent in-
tensified erosion by wind and water, would not erase the
marks which the great beasts had left upon their land.

The buffalo was a restrained and gentle user of the land and the grass . . . his grass, upon which the incredible growth and development of the herds depended. He ate it sparingly, grazing off only the tops of the stems, which grew as high as his magnificent head. The tops of the tender stalks contained the seedlings, the flavored nut, the storehouse of protein, and they waved there at the level of his maw. It was a reciprocal balance of favor. The buffalo spared the grass roots and left most of the stem for the protection of the new growth. In return, the grass replenished and fed upon itself in a perpetual cycle of abundance.

The great herds had vanished, but not so long ago. Thirty years earlier, there had been a few remnant groups scattered through the Milk River plataeu and hidden in the lower folds of the Little Rockies. All over that vast expanse the carcasses and the frequent mounds of bleaching bones gave mute testimony to the destructive efficiency of man. Even the herds of the Milk River country, sometimes filling the horizons, could not endure the slaughter. By packtrain, barge or wagon, mountains of hides had been carried to Williston or Mandan and then by flatboat down the Missouri to the leather factories of St. Louis. No respectable carriage in all America was wanting its buffalo robes. Nor was there anyone to suggest cropping the buffalo with specified kills each year. Americans were preoccupied with the squandering of their inheritance, and they went about it with energy and dispatch.

So the land had been left to the grass and its smaller denizens. The grass thrived and grew taller, forming an endless sea of seasonal green and gold; and in winter, it rose out of the snow to relieve the white monotony. Each blade and each stem, in consort with the winds sweeping down from the Canadian Northwest, sculptured on the snow surface its own minute drift, frosting the winterland with lacy musings of bas relief.

The spring wagon rolled northward through the sea of grass. Imperceptibly, the trail rose up toward the northern horizon. Each grade and rise was an introduction to another; each depression failed to dip as low as its predecessor. The great glacier had been a precise grade-maker, for all its awesome proportions, and a million thaws since had rounded and leveled the edges of the icecap's gougings.

As the grays slowed to a walk and reached the top of a short incline, the driver turned to point backward. "From the top of some of these hills you can see Saco at night," he said. "Way down there."

The young woman beside him turned in the high wagon seat and looked in the direction he had pointed. "Do we have a high hill?" she asked.

"There's one right behind where the house will be," he answered. Turning forward again, he shook the lines at the grays. "Now you can see where your neighbors live. That's Jim Mole's place just ahead, and the shack up there beyond and over to the west is Uncle Johnny's."

"Oh yes! Uncle Johnny! How are they?" she asked.

"Fine," he replied. "Aunt Em wanted us to stop by, but I thought you'd rather go on."

"Oh yes," she said. "Let's get to the ranch! I want to see it first."

"Only two miles now. You'll see what there is of it from the next hill. Now you can see Verbeck's shack. He built it out of sod . . . a bachelor. North of him are the two Pinkerman brothers . . ."

"You said in your letter, I think, that they both had families."

"Yeh," he replied. "I think they both have two kids."

"Have you met all these people?"

"No," he answered. "I met the Pinkermans the other day and Jim Mole here, but everybody's too busy to do much visiting . . . unless you have to borrow something."

"How are they about lending and helping?" she asked. "Are they helping each other?"

"Oh sure. We'll all have to help each other. The trouble is that everyone has shown up at the same time and everyone needs the same tools all at once . . . and everybody's busy."

She had leaned forward to peer into and tuck the blankets around a small bundle at her feet.

It was March 1913. My mother and I were arriving at the ranch. Dad had driven the grays and the spring wagon into Saco to meet us and bring us to what would be HOME!

The northern reaches of Montana had just been opened to settlement by the federal government under the Homestead Act. Washington had been prodded, beguiled, pressured and wooed into the decision by the indefatigable James J. Hill, builder of the Great Northern Railway. The Great Northern was conceived too late. Its application for charter was filed after the federal government's enthusiastic generosity in behalf of the earlier railroad builders had waned, and the latecomers were denied the alternating sections of land on each side of the rights of way.

The habit of the land-grant railroads, established by Congress in 1851, was originally meant to encourage construction of the Illinois Central, linking Chicago, Galena and Cairo. Congress gave the company 2,500,-000 acres of land. By 1884 the railroad land grants had reached an estimated total of 155,504,994 acres, an area almost the size of Texas. The Union Pacific had received 20,000,000 acres; the Santa Fe, 17,000,000; the Central and Southern Pacific, 24,000,000; the Northern Pacific, 44,000,000. Some of the Western states, ebullient over the prospects of railroad communication with the East, granted the new lines an additional 49,000,000 acres. By 1917, the Northern Pacific, striking a southern route through North Dakota and Montana, had realized $136,000,000 from the sales of some of its land.

The railroads racing for the Pacific Coast were also granted federal loans totaling $64,623,512, which were repaid with interest by 1899.

In return for all this federal generosity, the land-grant railroads agreed to transport United States property and troops at no cost. That agreement was later adjusted to 50 percent of normal commercial rates. On October 1, 1946, the low rates for government passengers and freight were discontinued entirely.

So Jim Hill built his "high line" across the top of the nation with investors' money and loans. He seized control of the bankrupt St. Paul and Pacific and pushed on through the extreme Northwest, reaching the Coast at Seattle in 1893. To guarantee the economic future of his enterprise and with no grants of public land, Jim Hill prevailed upon Washington to open the Montana area to homesteading so that he might promote farm settlement. He would haul the produce to the Eastern markets and bring back the hardware, groceries, machinery and all the endless necessities of the new farms and ranches.

As the Milk River and Missouri Bend territory was opened to settlement, the seekers of the land and the dreamers of dreams, the adventurers and the restless began to appear at the makeshift land offices in the towns and villages along Hill's railroad: in Cut Bank, Havre, Dodson, Malta, Saco, Hinsdale, Glasgow, Ft. Peck, Scobey and at a hundred other sidings and townsites, from the Rockies eastward into North Dakota and southward to the Missouri River and beyond.

Between 1870 and 1900, the area had been a vast cattle empire, the open range shared by four great brands: Phillips, Phelps, Matador and Coburn. They had fought the coming of the "squatter" and "sodbuster" with all their fury. Their cattle had grazed over an area 150 miles from east to west—100 miles from north to south. Previously, for how many centuries, these were the hunting grounds of the Assiniboin, the Gros Ventres or "Big Bellies," the Sioux, an occasional band of Crees and Chippewas, and sometimes the Nez Perce and Blackfeet.

But now it was 1913, and the glittering prize of free land had stirred my father, as it had beckoned to hundreds of thousands of other Americans. Land for the asking! Land for the taking! No nation, no government in all history had ever offered its citizens such a bonanza.

My father, together with my mother's father and Grandpa's brother, formed a loose compact to claim 960 acres of the new land. Consequently, my father left his employment with the Northern Pacific Railroad as a railroad telegrapher to reap his fortune from the land. He had journeyed to Saco and to the ranch site early in 1913 to help Grandpa construct a rude house which would shelter us until time and profit might permit the building of the grand ranch house.

Grandpa was a dealer and trader in assorted information and knowledge about Western land. He knew good land when he saw it, and he could detect value in it which was not always apparent to others. His love of the soil and the obvious satisfaction he took from making it produce, however, were in constant turmoil with his restless urgings for new frontiers. Breaking new sod was more thrilling than cultivating old land. Building a new house was more rewarding than living in a completed one. He derived a certain sense of satisfaction from hardship. New land and new frontiers had called to him all his adult life. He had brought his frail and diminutive wife and two small daughters westward from Missouri to Colorado in a covered wagon shortly before the turn of the century. He had explored and traded lands in Colorado and then gone on northward to Montana, forever listening to rumors about land . . . new land!

Grandpa had made at least two small fortunes by this time, but on each occasion he had taken his bankroll to Kansas City, moved into the Muehlebach Hotel, lived in a whirl of gaiety and reckless spending for a while, and then, with no regret, he went on to some new and challenging territory when his money was gone.

The March winds blew themselves into exhaustion, and the northland prepared to welcome April. Small, dainty, white daisies appeared in the shelter of the rocks on the hillsides. The sun grew warmer. At night the sky was vibrant with the whirring of unseen wings and the honking and calling of the great flights as they journeyed northward to the lakes and the muskeg of Canada.

The vast land was awakening, disturbed, this spring, by a multitude of new sights and sounds. The crisp morning air was filled with the remote intrusions of hammering, sawing, clanking and shouting as the new-comers arrived, threw their shacks together and hurled themselves at the virgin land. The road in front of our section grew busy with the traffic of wagons hauling lumber, farm machinery and household furnishings. New buildings—houses, shacks, barns and sheds—appeared on the landscape. A few "sodbusters" from the Dakotas and Nebraska, venturing out to new land, brought with them a custom from those areas and built dwellings out of the black sod. These earthen houses might or might not have floors, the roofs were usually of sod or tar paper, and the walls were blocks of grass-reinforced earth . . . cool in summer, warm and snug in winter, impervious to the wind and frost, and durable as granite. In most cases the sod houses were later transformed into chicken coops or cellars when the ranchers had time and the means to build their permanent dwellings.

They came from all parts of the nation, a few from Canada, some from Europe! Lou and Levi Osier from Quebec; George Glasscock from somewhere back East; the Otto Busches; and Andrew Strommen, a towering red-headed Norwegian, and his young bride, Coral, from Minnesota. To the west of us the Hans Waals, from Norway; the Ray Carters; Andrew Hanson, a bachelor straight from Norway; and down on the lower Whitewater, a family from czarist Russia. To the south of us, Uncle Johnny and Aunt Em (he was Grandpa's brother); the Jim Moles; the Jim Franklins and their brood of children; the two Sommers brothers and a sister (Art, Oscar and Emma), and Art's wife, Ada, from Wisconsin; and the McKee Andersons from Iowa. To the east, the Pinkermans from Nebraska; Louis Verbeck; and the Kapple family. A little beyond, to the southeast, the Pewonkies from Poland; and directly to the south in the river bottom, the Paalm family from Norway. And beyond them more families with strange names, and some with strange ways from strange and unfamiliar places of the nation and the world.

The list of projects was endless, persistently tugging at the mind, but the land had priority. Barns, sheds, fences, wells and housing could wait. The land would not. The cycle of plowing, disking, harrowing and planting permitted no flexibility and was intolerant of convenience. The seed had to be in the ground to take advantage of April's showers and May's warm sunshine. When the wheat and oats were planted, time enough then to provide for the comforts of men and animals.

My father was an apt pupil. From Grandpa he learned how to harness the horses and operate the farm machines. He watched the plowshares sink deeply into the grass sod and turn the furrows like curling waves of dark water. At his feet, the sharp rotating disks bit hungrily into the rows of sod, leaving behind a smooth

bed of soil. Behind the harrow and drag, only his foot-
prints marred the soft, inviting seedbed. The drill
turned the fields into an endless series of subtle furrows, the small ridges containing the seed, and the delicate depressions acting as trenches for the water.

All of Dad's energies and his boundless enthusiasm
were now directed toward the flowering of the land . . .
HIS LAND! From the fields he glanced toward the
small tar-papered hut at the bottom of the hill. He did
not see its meager proportions nor its ugly façade. He
envisioned, instead, a stately two-story house peering
through tall willows and poplars, the dormer windows,
the spacious front porch, and a white picket fence surrounding a green lawn. To the left of the house he
saw a great red barn with adjoining sheds, granary, corral, and towering over all a sparkling windmill
hurling shafts of light from its blades. They were magnificent dreams, unblighted, untouched by despair.

Dad was in the fields early in the morning and
barely allowed himself and the horses an hour for
lunch, which was universally known as dinner. The
evening meal was supper. He left the fields—weary,
sweat-stained and hungry—only when the long twi-
light was ending and darkness crept over the soft hills.

Grandpa too must have had his dreams, but he never
revealed them. It was as though he had been through
all of this before, and he had. He never wished out
loud, nor invoked hope. He provided, therefore, a measure of strength for the others with his attitude of confidence: put work and labor into the soil, and by some
immutable law it would offer its own apodictic reward.

There was no mystery about the land with him. It was a producer of grains and fruits, but it required taming, controlling, and some bending to his gigantic but quiet will. Grandpa kept Dad's enthusiasms and impatience within bounds, arranged the calendar and the schedule of projects in behalf of an orderly progression toward first things first.

While Dad worked the fields, Grandpa undertook the other assorted tasks and chores. He went to the spring down near the river once or twice a week to fill and bring back in the farm wagon the brimming barrels of fresh water. He went somewhere, one day, and returned with a cow and heifer calf. Every two weeks or so he made the long trip into town and came back with the wagon overflowing: groceries and household appliances per written orders and precise specifications of Mother and Grandma, coal, articles of clothing, machinery, spare parts, a crate of baby chicks, seed, tools, all the newly arrived packages from Sears Roebuck and "Monkey" Ward, and a couple pints of whiskey. Grandpa had to hide the whiskey somewhere about the ranch, because Grandma would "raise Cain" if she found it in the house. If he nipped at it judiciously, it would last until the next trip to town.

Wood was a precious commodity. From a high hill we could look out over the immense land to the jumble of the Larb Hills south of Saco, westward to the Little Rockies shimmering through the intervening hundred miles like a steel-blue saw blade, and east and north to some indefinite point where earth and sky blended into a vague horizon. And over all that vast distance, not a single tree or shrub disturbed the luxurious monotony of the grass. Hidden from sight were the fringes of box elder and an occasional clump of willows along Stinky Creek and the Whitewater. The Milk River flowed through generous groves of willows, poplar, cottonwood and box elder, but they were concealed in the narrow valley.

Occasionally, Dad or Grandpa took a team and wagon to the river or to one of the creeks and returned at night with a load of kindling wood. However, the wood problem was one that the ranch solved by itself. As more cattle were placed on the grassland and put to graze on the unclaimed public lands nearby, we adopted the ways of the Indians who frequently camped for a night or two on our ranch. The sunbleached and weathered droppings of the cattle made a splendid and incredibly hot fuel. One of my first childhood chores was to take a team and the wagon, drive through the range land, and return with tremendous loads of what we called "cow chips." Frontiersmen had used buffalo manure for their fuel, as did the Indians, and they called the dried fiberlike piles "buffalo chips."

Finally the crops were in the ground, and there was nothing remaining for human energy, skill or adeptness. The fate of a new frontier hung breathless upon the capricious weather.

The first whim of the weather gods was a benevolent one. A few days after the planting was completed, dark and low-hanging clouds came in by night and turned the morning into a sodden, gray mist. All day the rain came down gently and without pause. Then in the early evening it ceased and the setting sun shot its rays, triumphantly, under the cloud cover and onto the drenched land . . . a sure omen of a warm and sunny tomorrow. In the dank, dark womb of the soil the seeds stirred and began to burgeon.

The next and now vital project was the digging of a well, a task approached with an air of suspense; for without a reliable source of water, this great hope and promising venture would become a mockery. Disquieting reports had come that some of the neighboring ranches were having serious trouble locating underground water. Grandpa, however, was confident that beneath the bottom land lay a great underground reservoir, fed by the drainage from the surrounding hills. The lake at the southern extremity of the basin area was a sign that below the ground lay a subterranean storehouse of water.

A transient water diviner had appeared at the shack one day, indicating that he was doing a brisk business throughout the area, but Grandpa curtly informed the latter-day sorcerer to stop wasting his time—that he would "do no business here!"

Divining for water was a superstitious notion that had come from Europe by way of England. It was sometimes called "witching for water" or "bending for water." The druidic art consisted of the soothsayer or diviner and a willow branch of precisely the right length, girth, weight and age. Presumably, the hydraulic priest had in these unrevealed specifications a built-in alibi for a possible repeat performance should he fail the first time around. He could always declare that the local willows were just not up to standard. In any event, the diviner walked slowly, swinging the willow branch back and forth; and if he possessed any histrionic artfulness, he murmured strange and impressive incantations. If the willow bent slowly to the ground, that spot marked the presence of a modest supply of water. If the willow dipped suddenly or violently, it indicated a veritable underground Niagara. The going rate for all of this was what the fast-talking expert thought the traffic would bear, conditioned by how desperate he thought the homesteader might be.

The excavation began a few feet from the shack and slightly above the designated area for the barns and the outhouse. It was beastly, miserable, backbreaking work. The diameter of a well had to be modest, preferably about four feet, else it would have a tendency to cave in. The workman was cramped into four feet of space at the bottom of a deep hole in the ground. He had little room to swing a pick or secure an efficient grip on the shovel. A windlass was rigged above the hole to hoist up the dirt. The workman could ascend and descend on the windlass, if it was sufficiently strong; or he might lower a long ladder into the shaft.

The work went slowly and painfully in spite of the fact that both Grandpa and Dad concentrated on it.

They reached fifteen feet, twenty feet, twenty-five, then thirty, and Grandpa's growing concern became obvious. They might dig another ten feet, and if there was no water at that depth they would be forced to try somewhere else, for at anything more than forty feet the pump would be too difficult to operate. Down another five feet they dug, and yet another five. Nothing! The first disappointment and the bitter taste of dismay on the tongue.

Without pausing to refill the hole, they chose a new site: about a hundred and fifty yards or so toward the center of the basin. Grandma hurriedly covered the dry well with boards to prevent her chickens or the calf falling down the shaft. Again the work was laborious and galling, and again they brought back to the shack each day their ill-concealed anxiety.

But one day as they came in for the noon meal their attitudes were jauntier. They had hit a trickle of water at twenty-five feet. The next day the work was slower. The earth at the bottom of the shaft was wet and heavy, and water had to be bailed out frequently. As they dug deeper, however, the water failed to increase its flow. At thirty-five feet it was still only a trickle, and again at forty feet it was clear that they had labored in vain. Dark and foreboding possibilities weighed upon them. What if some freakish underground formation of rock and earth were draining the moisture and sending it into some inaccessible subterranean cavern or pool? Could the whole basin be but a hanging crust of earth over some vast hidden sink?

Grandpa sat on the edge of the well at the end of that bitter day, wiped the sweat from his forehead with the back of a mud-caked hand, glanced up at Dad, and asked, "Do you suppose we'll have to send for that witch-doctor son-of-a-bitch after all?"

He arose and walked solemnly to the shack.

The third and now desperate try was made two hundred fifty yards to the south of the shack, a long way to carry water should they find it; but by now water at any distance would be accepted without question. Again the agonizing boring at the stubborn ground. The mound of black dirt beside the excavation grew higher. At twenty feet the ground was cool and moist, but it gave no sign of a flow. At twenty-five feet . . . still nothing!

Dad was taking his turn at the bottom. By this time he had surmounted the queasy discomfort of the darkness and loneliness at the bottom of the deep pit. Suddenly he shouted to the top, "Bob, I think we've got it!"

"How much is it flowing?" asked Grandpa, as he peered into the shaft.

"At one place here it's running out pretty fast!" was the muffled reply.

"Come on up!" Grandpa shouted.

He put on a pair of hip boots and descended into the well. "If we've hit water," he said, "we'll have to work fast to get as much dirt out of the bottom as we can."

Presently he called that he was coming up. The water was creeping toward the top of his boots!

This was a generous land.

Dad was born and reared in an old Wisconsin mill-town, deserted by the lumbering industry, which had moved on to the big pines and firs of the Northwest. His father had been a skilled woodworker, furniture maker, builder of canoes, and had been employed at a factory, making carriages. Albert Huntley was the skilled craftsman who, with delicate brushes, painted the narrow darts on the spokes of the wheels and the gold medallions and red flourishes on the bodies. He worked the wood and applied the glistening finishes.

One of seven children, Dad had attended primary school and worked at a wide assortment of odd jobs, but the family economics made it mandatory that he strike out for himself at the earliest opportunity.

Dad's Christian name, imposed upon him by a well-meaning mother, had been something to overcome. It was Percy Adams Huntley. The Adams would not have been too bad, had they chosen to call him that. It signified descendancy from the proud Revolutionary family of Massachusetts. But Percy! There was no way to get around that! Dad, upon being asked, would simply say that his name was "Purse." So he was known, until later years, when for some unknown reason he became "Pat."

When he was nineteen, Dad left Wisconsin and journeyed West. An older sister had married a railroad telegrapher on the Northern Pacific, and Dad stopped off to visit for a few days. His brother-in-law taught him telegraphy, and Dad found himself a young railroad telegrapher on the N.P.

At Springdale, Montana, he met my mother, the belle of the valley. She had taught school for a short while. She thought nothing of riding horseback or driving a buckboard fifteen or twenty miles to a Saturday night dance. Mother's hair was her crowning endowment. It was light brown with a faint tint of red, and when she let it down around her shoulders it fell in soft undulating waves to her knees. One of my earliest childhood memories is the vision of my mother combing and brushing her long hair.

The young operator at Springdale and Bob Tatham's daughter fell in love. Dad was transferred to Columbus, forty-five miles or so eastward, and he rode the trains, passenger and freight, back and forth to see the girl who lived at Springdale.

In December 1910 they were married in Billings, and they went to see a performance of *The Chocolate Soldier* that night.

I was born a year later. Dad was then stationed at Cardwell, Montana. In most of the smaller stations along the line, the Northern Pacific provided living quarters for the agent in the rear of the depot. I was born in a Northern Pacific depot!

The railroad labor unions were young at that time and had not won the gains which they would achieve in later years. All organized labor was in its infancy, and it was a sickly and unpromising child. The wages paid by the railroads were about standard, probably a little below the average for the industrial North. But it was a time when young Americans were cautioned against "working for someone else." If you wanted to get ahead, you must do it on your own. There were opportunities everywhere.

The railroads, and the covered wagons before them, had opened the last sections of the West. American industry was beginning to warm up to its incredibly productive pace, and the American system of distribution, one of the world's wonders of sophisticated economic articulation, was beginning to function. In spite of recurring depressions and economic slumps, Americans were buying and producing and building and moving goods. In all this growth and activity there were places for everyone, and with any luck a man could find that niche for himself. It was the golden age of American capitalism. It implied that every man was his own boss . . .

Furthermore, there was the old American sentimentality about the land. There was a particular and special virtue about the 160-acre farm. Life on the farm . . . on the land . . . was in the American image. The growing cities of the nation were places of dirt and sin and foreigners. The nation's virtue . . . "white, Anglo-Saxon, Protestant virtue" . . . was thought to spring from the land, from the 160-acre farm.

In addition, the farmland of the Midwest had produced a glut of food, and the tillers of that tremendous section of America had thrived and prospered. In every town and village of the Midwest, the successful farmer was admired and envied; and this attitude toward the land was carried westward.

For all these reasons Dad had responded to Grandpa's suggestion that they consider the opportunity in the Milk River country. Here the government was offering not 160 acres, but twice that!

Mother discovered it: the first promise. As they arose one morning and were enduring the daily awkwardness of raising and lowering improvised curtain partitions and otherwise making some effort to observe the rudiments of modesty, Mother chanced to glance out the window. She looked again and uttered a short cry of disbelief. It could be no mirage or some trick of the rising sun! Where the cultivated fields had been great patches of dark brown the day before, now they were unmistakably green!

The omnibus of tasks and projects weighed heavily on those crowded weeks of the first summer. Barns and sheds and chicken coops still had to be built; the entire section, one mile square, had to be fenced with four miles of wire, and the pasture land separated from the cultivated fields by another mile of it. The garden and the yard around the chosen location for the house had to be enclosed (Mother said she was not going to have young calves and colts wandering about the parlor!). A fine crop of hay for the coming winter was cut from the grassland in the bottom and from some of the swales in the west "three-twenty." Harvest season was coming on and a granary had to be built. Grandpa bought another team of horses, at a reduced price because they were unbroken. These animals, Rex and Savage, a pair of tremendous, barrel-chested, gray geldings, would journey to France, one day, in the service of the United States Army as artillery horses. They had to be tamed to the bit and harness . . . and the harness and wagon had to be repaired after Rex and Savage had scattered it over a good part of the landscape. Dad and Grandpa returned from a livestock sale in town with three more heifers and a pair of saddle horses.

There was also the farm machinery, to be constantly maintained and repaired. The livestock had to be tethered each evening lest it wander off over the unfenced range or eat up half the grain crop. Grandma had to keep her chickens in old packing cases. It was such a distance to the well that Grandpa rigged a "stone boat" —a platform on stout runners which a horse could pull over the ground—on which two barrels of water could be transported to the house.

Grandpa was the repairer and builder. Dad never did quite master the mysteries of the brace-and-bit, the level, anvil and chisel. In his hands they were stubborn and unmanageable instruments, but Grandpa could coax iron, steel, wire or wood to take the shape and function of his will. He could repair alarm clocks, make violins, deliver colts and nurse sick or injured animals back to health. People, the land, animals and machinery all responded to his quiet and indomitable command. Those around him borrowed reassurance from the confidence he had in his own strength. With his firm verbal urgings and his touch on the lines he forded the Milk River repeatedly in wagons loaded with tons of steel pipe or lumber and with teams of eight, ten or twelve semibroken horses in every conceivable kind of hitch. Depending on the configuration of the hitch, he might tie one pair of lines around his neck, another around his waist, and slip the others, in pairs, between his fingers.

The years of sun and wind had tanned Grandpa's lean face, adding intensity to his gray eyes. For all his six-foot-two frame and broad shoulders, he probably weighed no more than a hundred eighty pounds. He was the unquestioned champion of the dance floor, executing the varied maneuvers of the square dance and quadrille with graceful flourishes or leading his partner through the smooth glidings of the waltz.

The weather held, blessing the land with alternating showers and days of sunshine. The wheat field became a great carpet of dark green, the oats sparkled in a lighter shade, and the surrounding hills and prairie sported their new grass.

On the Fourth of July that first year, the garden yielded fresh peas, green onions, radishes, leaf lettuce and new potatoes. Grandma's brood of chickens gave up the first friers.

One day a stranger rode up to the ranch and introduced himself as the owner of a threshing machine. He
had been expected. He said he would be back with his
equipment in about two weeks, that he was starting on
the north side of the Milk and would work northward,
ranch by ranch. Dad and Grandpa could make their
own arrangements about the harvesting crew, deciding
with which neighbors they would exchange help. The
visitor admired the stands of wheat and oats, said he
would take his pay in grain or cash, and rode off.

Dad and Grandpa negotiated the brief communal
harvest pact with the Pinkermans and Levi Osier. They
brought their teams, the big hayracks mounted atop
the farm wagons, and their wives and children. The
wives were laden with pots and pans and jars filled
with prepared food. Then, when the thresher moved on
to the Pinkermans' and Osiers', the process was re-
versed . . . our teams, racks, men, wives, children,
cakes, pies and roasts went to their places.

The harvest was in and it was a generous one! A few
bushels of wheat were reserved for the chickens and
for seed. There were more than enough oats for the
horses. The sideboards were put on the wagon, it was
filled to the brim, and the first load was taken to the
elevator in Saco.

With the initial check, the various accounts at the

stores in town were settled. No one paid up until harvest time.

Grandma Tatham was a precious little soul. Among all the cherished memories of her there is not one in which she was ever resting or sitting still or just idling. Her tiny hands were forever flying: mending, crocheting, darning, knitting, ironing, churning, paring or rolling dough. Her small and delicate little body was in constant motion, but without flutter. There was a purpose for every movement.

Life on the new land was difficult, and it precluded most women from maintaining a consistent degree of personal tidiness. There was little justification, and far less time, to groom the hair, apply creams to face and hands, or take pains with dresses and aprons. Grandma, however, never yielded her fastidiousness. I can remember her dexterous manipulation of the curling iron as she applied it to the small locks of hair around her face. The iron was heated inside a lamp chimney. Frequently, she placed small leather-covered curlers in her hair at night. Her dresses were immaculately ironed and pressed, her blouses and aprons crisply starched, her button shoes were shined.

Grandma's family in the small Missouri town where she was born and reared had been "well off." Her father owned a number of farms, and he worked them expertly. The Waldens were definitely the "upper crust" of the community.

Grandpa, on the other hand, came from the wrong side of the tracks. He was born in the last year of the Civil War into an incredibly large family of boys. His father died when he was very young, and his mother later married a widower who had several young sons of his own. In such an environment of brothers and step-brothers, Grandpa learned that survival went to the quick and the strong. He learned to defend himself. The Tatham and Thorp boys were the juvenile delinquents of the town. If they were not responsible for every misdeed, they were blamed for it, nonetheless.

Grandma's family interposed strong objections when she announced that she was going to marry Bob Tatham, but Frances Walden was not deterred. I would assume that her dark eyes flashed defiance and she went ahead quietly with her plans.

Her eyes were incredibly expressive. They could chastise, weep without tears, or laugh; they could fill with sorrow or overflow with joy and gladness. They could snap sharp commands. Grandma was the one whom a small boy tried most to please. Her praise and her commendation were like magnificent blessings.

She could have been no stranger to anxiety and despair, but she gave little sign of it to her two daughters or to anyone else. She endured her husband's reckless holidays in Kansas City, she made few inquiries about bank account or family fortune. She was confident that her tall, lean man would return and would provide . . . and somehow he did. She was aware that his love was abiding, if not constant; and she forgave him because he was the boy with a little streak of "wildness" who needed just some more "bringing up."

Vividly, I can see Grandpa lifting Grandma into and out of buggies and wagons. He would place his great hands around her frail little waist, she would place her hands on his, and he would lift her high and effortlessly in a swirl of skirts and petticoats.

Many years later in Los Angeles, when he was ninety-two and she had been dead for thirty-five years, Grandpa tossed down his drink of whiskey, neat, and turned to me. "How well do you remember Franny?" he asked.

"Grandma?" I said.

"Yes."

"Oh, I remember much about her, Grandpa. I remember her eyes, how neat she was. I remember her making hot biscuits every morning, seven days a week . . . and not out of ready-mix, either!"

"That's right," he smiled. "I haven't had a decent biscuit in thirty-five years."

I ordered another brace of whiskies. Grandpa took his and went to the window, where he stood looking out over the valley below. He contemplated the whiskey a long time and said, "You know, I could put my hands all the way around her waist. She was so tiny . . . and so dear."

Other seasons came and went. The cycles of preparing the ground, planting, praying a bit and harvesting were repeated. The fences, barn, sheds and the house were constructed.

The shack was given an exterior of ship lath over the tar paper, and it became the kitchen and dining area. Onto the north side two stories were added: a large living room and a bedroom downstairs, more bedrooms upstairs. Since there was no basement, only the root cellar beneath the kitchen, the house sat almost on the ground, and Dad's high front porch had to be sacrificed; but as a compromise, Grandpa built a low porch floor which extended from the front of the house onto the yard about eight feet. A roof and the supporting pillars for it could come later.

What is surely my first memory was the absence of Mother for a while and then her return with a small incomprehensible thing, which, I was told, was my sister. My companion, my confidante, my patient, understanding and forgiving Wadine.

I cannot remember when Shep appeared. It seemed to me that he was always there. Out of my own experience, I have subscribed to everything ever said about a boy and his dog, particularly a farm boy.

Shep was an uncertain mixture of shepherd and collie, and I have no sure recollection just how handsome he really was. I recall that his nose was cold, his tongue was warm and friendly on my hands and face, and his fur was made for a small boy to grasp and cling to through romp and roughhouse.

Remembered also are brief instances of fright . . . momentary fear . . . when the lamplight in the little unfinished ranch house revealed dark faces peering through the windowpanes. The whites of eyes were like small luminous orbs in the blackness. Driven by insatiable curiosity about these newcomers to the land where they had hunted, an occasional group of Assiniboin would pay their visit. In the daytime they sat silently on their horses and watched us as we went about the chores. At night they studied us from the darkness, little concerned whether they were detected, and obviously concluding that if the white man insisted on windows in his lodge he must expect the passer-by to look inside. The Indians did us no harm. They only baffled us with their stoicism and imperturbable countenances.

Apparently the Indians had made it clear that communication between themselves and these intruders would be a long and tedious process. The settlers accepted it and made little effort to exchange more than the nod of the head or the universal signal of peaceful intent, which was no more than the raising of one hand. The Indians were in no haste to learn the white man's language, and they were in less haste to use it. The settlers' efforts to converse usually ended in frustration and a kind of embarrassment, for the Indian's response was a detached stare at the horizon or at some vague point just above the rancher's head. It was too soon. Sitting Bull was less then a quarter century dead. On the reservations the old warriors still spun their tales of the last battles, and precious were the legacies of vicarious pride from the exploits of Chief Gall, Crazy Horse, Chief Joseph and the others. A half century later, even in the 1960s, communication between Indian and white man would sometimes falter.

An Indian, searching for stray horses, sat astride his wiry little pony one morning, talking to Dad and Grandpa at the corral gate. A white beaded headband held his long black hair in place, a handsome blanket fell casually from his shoulders. His lean legs were encased in tight-fitting trousers, and his moccasined feet hung easily alongside his horse's belly.

The Indian did Grandpa the customary courtesy of asking for a pipeful of tobacco, for which a "thank you" was never given and never expected. Between puffs on his pipe, the Indian said that the signs told of a mild winter . . . the badgers were dark in color and no white wolves had been seen. Abruptly he turned his horse and trotted off. Conversations with the Indians were refreshingly free of small talk.

Several years later a small Indian band, including two boys my age, rode up to the ranch house as I was engaged in the repair of a halter. They watched me intently as I put the rivets through the leather and rounded them off with a hammer on the anvil. One of the boys returned to his horse and removed the beaded and ornamented hackamore. Half in sign language and half in broken English, he offered to trade his hackamore for my halter plus one dollar. I can recall Grandpa and the other Indians watching and listening with great concentration as the Indian lad and I bargained. Finally I closed the deal with an emphatic gesture of one index finger at the half-joint of the other, and the Indian boy nodded. The Indians smiled in appreciation, and Grandpa, with a great laugh, handed to me a half dollar.

Our horses, however, never responded satisfactorily to the hackamore; they were too accustomed to the bridle and bit. I often watched and admired the Indian boys as they demonstrated their horsemanship. Once or twice I encountered them on the open range land and we raced our mounts. They sat high on their horses' shoulders, almost at the base of the neck, and leaned precariously over the flying mane. They never jeered at my comparatively awkward riding talent, but they were frankly contemptuous of my saddle and bridle. It was clear that it seemed funny to them that this white boy insisted on placing a saddle in the middle of a horse and riding back there where all the bouncing occurred.

The traffic accidents of those days were runaway horses. I was a horrified witness to a number of them . . . a participant in several.

The demand for horses was considerable among the new farmers. It was a seller's market. Consequently, the livestock dealers had no time in which to break the horses to harness or to the farm implements, and the homesteader was equally short of time and frequently more short of skill. The result was that the prairie roads abounded with semiwild horses attached to buggies, spring wagons and farm vehicles. Too often the horses attempted to get themselves unattached, and their average was remarkable.

The magnificent Rex and Savage were what my grandmother called "highly spirited." My grandfather called them "crazy gray sons-a-bitches." They were more or less predictable until they met another rig. Residing somewhere in their great heads and chests was a furious hatred for automobiles, which occasionally sputtered and bounded along the lanes. Rex and Savage would detect a car or another rig approaching, emit a series of warning snorts, shake their heads against the restraint of the lines and bits, then arch their necks and begin to run. Faster and faster they flew toward their detested target! The spring wagon leaped over the bumps as it crossed and recrossed the deep ruts. Dad or Grandpa, or both, braced their feet against the dash, pulled on the lines until they threatened to snap, and shouted every known variety of imprecation—but the horses ran faster! Our neighbors, aware of the unstable habits of Rex and Savage, would pull hastily off the road and wait in terror as the two beasts bore down upon them. The team charged straight and unerringly toward the advancing rig, and then, at the very last fraction of a second, veered sharply away and avoided the other vehicle by an eyelash. Frequently, the terrified rancher stood up, waved his whip and shouted something about getting "that damn team off the road!" Within a couple hundred yards, Rex and Savage would decelerate to an impeccable walk, their show of authority ended.

Mother had grave misgivings about going into town with Dad behind the erratic team of grays. Finally, she succumbed to Dad's reassurances on the grounds that all the "steam" had been taken out of them by a week of heavy plowing.

The trip into town was uneventful, and we were on the way home, a mile or so north of the river, the spring wagon piled with groceries and bundles, when the team launched its assault against an oncoming rig. Bundles and packages flew out of the wagon bed.

Mother, anticipating disaster, held her hat with one hand and me with the other, somehow managing to climb over the wildly bouncing seat and make her way to the rear. Clutching me desperately, she slid over the endgate, let go, hit the ground with her feet and catapulted into a pinwheel of limbs, youngster and long skirts.

Rex and Savage made their "pass" at the offending vehicle and came to a halt. By the time Dad had turned around and driven back, the other driver was picking up some of Mother's dignity. The damage was slight—a few bruises and pride. Like any four-year-old, I had simply rolled and bounced.

Through a few uncontrolled tears, Mother laid down the ultimatum that never again would she ride behind that team of broncs. She insisted on walking the rest of the way home, but Dad finally prevailed upon her to get back in the wagon. However, she rode in the rear with the endgate removed so she could get out quickly.

One neighbor had a runaway on the road in front of the ranch. He was driving a team of fine blacks, which took fright or exception to something and began to run. The wagon shed a wheel, and it rolled, leaping and bouncing, up the lane. As the bare axle dug into the road it exerted a sudden pull to that side, catapulting the runaways into our fence! The driver was thrown out, the fence posts splintered off, the wire screeched as it was pulled through the staples; then it snapped and gave way, cutting a great gash across the chest of one of the horses. Now the team was genuinely out of all control. The horse with the injury screamed in pain, his chest gushing blood, and the animals charged across our wheat field, parts of the wagon flying off.

Grandpa, working in the adjoining field, ran at a tangent which might permit him to intercept the bolting horses, and as the team galloped past him, he lunged and caught one of the flying reins, turning the frantic animals slightly into a wide circle. Then he was able to grasp the side of the wagon and vault into it. With the team still galloping furiously, Grandpa slipped over the front of the wagon and out onto the tongue, clutching at the harnesses, until he could seize the bridles and gradually bring the frenzied, lathered animals to a halt.

Chet Huntley

Blood was surging down the legs of the wounded horse. Grandpa quickly unhitched him and led him to the barn. There he staunched the flow, stitched the gaping wound together and disinfected it with powder. In a few days, the grateful owner came and led his horse away.

Another runaway, this one on a road to the east of us, almost ended in disaster to the entire community. It was in the fall, when the grass had turned dry. As the team bolted up the road, a shoe on one of the horses or a tire on the wagon must have struck a spark from a stone. The teamster ultimately brought his horses under control and got out to assay the damage—but suddenly, in the direction from which the team had brought him, he noticed a wisp of smoke rising from the roadside. He turned about and raced to the spot but it was too late! A stiff east wind had caught the small flame and was sending it crackling through the tall grass!

Five miles or so away, we saw the cloud of smoke on the east horizon. Prairie fire!

On ranch after ranch the cry went up! It was a cry of anguish and terror which had been handed down from the Indians and the plainsmen. They had seen fire sweep over hundreds of miles of prairie, driving the great herds of buffalo, the coyotes, antelope and jack rabbits in front of it. Now it was real. Crops, pasture, farm buildings and livestock were menaced.

Men and women seized old articles of clothing and gunnysacks, leaped on horses and raced toward the towering cloud of smoke. Others hitched their teams to wagons, loaded them with barrels of water and drove toward the fire. Within an hour, the fire front was more than a mile long and it had advanced two miles westward. The fire fighters made a desperate stand around one ranch house, checked the flames around the small perimeter and then raced around the end of the line to get in front of the advance.

By dusk, the flames had reached the eastern lip of our ranch basin. Jim Pinkerman's buildings had been saved, but several head of cattle had perished when they were caught between the fire and a fence; and his west pasture was a great sea of leaping flame. The area over which the fire had passed was dense black against the contrasting gold of the unburned prairie. Here and there piles of manure continued to smoulder.

Darkness came on, and our whole eastern horizon was a wall of dancing fire. The line of crackling, fiendish death was now about five miles long. Our world . . . the safe, secure and changeless prairie . . . had been transformed into a nightmarish inferno creeping into our basin.

I had been left in the care of Grandma. Mother had joined Dad and Grandpa on the fire line. We stood in the front yard and watched the wavering crests of flame advance across Jim Pinkerman's pasture toward the road and our east fence. Grandma, tiny and delicate, stood with one hand to her cheek, never moving and saying nothing. The anxiety in her eyes commanded even a small boy to be silent. In the dusk, animals ran through the barnyard or paused for a moment in fright before the fence which ran around the yard. A fat badger waddled hurriedly up the hill behind the house. Jack rabbits leaped past. A small weasel scurried through the fence and darted out of sight, and a coyote skirted the buildings and slid into the half-light.

The army of fire fighters had decided to try to backburn along a line just inside our land. Quickly, they ignited a line and burned a strip about fifty yards deep. They extinguished that fire and took up positions to prevent the main fire from leaping over the burned-off strip. If they could control the shower of sparks and embers, they might halt the advance.

The wall of heat and smoke marched up to the burned-off strip. The fence posts caught fire and stood like small pillars of flame. It hesitated at the blackened strip.

Figures ran about in the darkness, beating at small fires touched off by flying embers. There were shouts and commands. From the house, Grandma and I could see the men and women racing back and forth, silhouetted against the fire. The flames faltered, made a few last desperate attempts to leap the barrier, and then began to die down.

The men, and some of the women, remained along the fire line all night and until early in the morning, for fear that the wind might increase and set the inferno rolling again.

But the wind receded and a new day flooded the prairie land . . . calm and still.

I have been unable to sort out the overlapping attitudes of respect and affection I had for the four adults who made up so much of my childhood. Grandma was the cherished one to whom I went for the ultimate in praise and the one I avoided when I had done something I should not have. She was the final authority on all matters of morality and behavior and manners. Mother was the beautiful repository of love and affection. Dad was the good-natured and tolerant companion rather than guide and counselor. Grandpa, however, was my heroic figure, and I spent much of those early years chasing at his heels.

I learned that Grandma and Mother were unsatisfactory sources of information about animal habits and ranch life. Frequently, I was informed that small boys had no need for answers to such questions. Dad too was something less than candid. But Grandpa told me what I wanted to know . . . bluntly and somewhat vividly. What I failed to learn from him, I picked up easily from the hired hands who worked on the ranch later. Somehow, every association with Grandpa held the promise or the possibility of high adventure.

He never realized, I suppose, what he did for the ego of a small boy when he waived aside the misgivings of Grandma and Mother and took me into town with him. Those were the moments of triumph!

Chet Huntley

Town was an intense and exciting concentration of sounds and sights and noises and smells—particularly, smells. The dry-goods stores were veritable bazaars of aroma: coffee (in barrels), boxes of dried fish, dried fruit in bulk, kerosene, spices, harnesses and saddles, and smoked meats. The drugstore, with its ice cream parlor in conjunction, was another establishment which sent its array of aromas out across the boardwalk and into the dusty street. There were all the scents of chemicals and medicines, but more powerful was the mouth-watering aroma of the ice cream soda. These odors and scents blended into those of the street, horse manure and harness.

The ice cream parlor and drugstore had its own characteristic sounds and appearances too. The furniture invariably sported elaborately curved metal legs. The seats of the chairs were wooden or sometimes wicker. As the metal legs of the chairs scraped on the floor they created a sound unlike that anywhere else, and the soda faucet hissed and coughed deliciously as it squirted a foaming stream of nectar into the cone-shaped container.

On rare occasions in these recent years, I have driven into some small Western town and detected just a trace of that heady combination of aromas— harness, saddle leather, saddle soap and manure; bulk coffee, ice cream soda and kerosene—and I can hear the shouts of the teamsters around the livery stable, the sound of boots and heavy farm shoes on the wooden sidewalks, the jangle of tug chains; and see the dust on Main Street, with the row of storefronts on one side, the Great Northern tracks, the depot and the grain elevators on the other.

Grandpa would place the order at the dry-goods store, then run his errands at the drugstore, the shoe-repair shop, perhaps stop at the bank or the farm-machinery showroom, and collect the mail at the post office. We would have lunch at the counter of a café or grill. That was always a great experience. I never could deduce how Grandpa made our selection so rapidly and conclusively from the myriad offerings on the menu. To the disgust of Grandma and Mother, I thought restaurant food was the finest one could imagine.

The orders placed and the errands completed, Grandpa had a little time for the last and crowning transaction of the day, before getting the team out of the livery stable, picking up the purchases and starting the long drive home. He paid his respects at the saloon!

Another cloud of strange aromas lay behind the swinging doors and the opaque windows: the heady scent of whiskey and stale tobacco smoke. As Grandpa leaned his elbows on the bar, rested one foot on the brass rail, pushed back his hat and exchanged pleas-antries with the bartender, I would anticipate the white-aproned proprietor's reach for the ice vat in which, I knew, he kept the most fantastically delicious liquid substance the world had ever known: straw-berry soda pop! It occurred to me that Grandpa drank something slightly different. It came out of a larger bottle, which the proprietor merely placed on the bar with a small glass; but I thought Grandpa's drink was sufficiently similar to mine that I had tremendous admiration for his taste and his unbounding wisdom in knowing where these things were available.

Grandpa would satisfy his thirst, buy a couple pints for consumption at the ranch, and we would leave in time to arrive home by dusk and the supper hour.

One trip into town with Grandpa was climactic. He had concluded the various errands and made his customary call at the saloon. It was Saturday afternoon, and there were more customers in the establishment than usual. Grandpa was savoring the aftertaste of his whiskey, and I had taken my bottle of soda to a chair on the other side of the room. An ugly, squat, bull-necked and frightfully powerful man made his way along the bar and stood glowering at Grandpa.

Instinctively, I knew we were in for trouble. I had heard stories about "Rip," and it was obvious that this was he.

Rip was the town bully and terror. He operated a sometime dray or delivery service, and the saloon was his home and office. Rip's chief ambition was to terrorize the town and boast that he had licked or intimidated every man in the area. He was a thoroughly detested beast, and the town was in the process of petitioning the sheriff to chase him out and get rid of him, once and for all.

Rip looked Grandpa up and down, and with a snarl asked, "Are you Bob Tatham?"

I shrank in fright into the back of my chair, trying to look as small and inconspicuous as possible. I also elected a refuge under the pool table in the event things should develop as I had reason to think they might.

Grandpa put down his glass, turned slowly and surveyed his man. "Yes, I'm Bob Tatham," he answered.

"Tatham," sneered Rip, "You've got quite a reputation around here, d'ya know that? They tell me you're quite a fightin' man."

The bartender leaned over the bar and made a feeble effort to intercede. "Now, look here, Rip. Let's not have any trouble. Why don't you just go about your business—"

He was cut short by the persistent challenger. "Mind your business behind the bar, Shorty, you little bastard, I've got me a great big fightin' man."

Grandpa turned and I could see him coiling to avoid any sudden blow. "Rip," he said slowly, "I'm not lookin' for any trouble with you, but if you insist on it, you're gonna' have your hands full."

Rip backed up and the men at the bar stepped aside and retreated toward the rear of the saloon. I slid out of my chair and crouched at the far side of the pool table. Rip lowered his head, clenched his great hairy fists, roared like an enraged lion and charged.

Grandpa's fist wasn't enough to stop the battering-ram assault, but he deflected it. Rip went halfway down, and his head butted Grandpa against the bar. I was now peering out from under the pool table—a thoroughly frightened five-year-old.

Rip shook his head from the blow, backed off and charged again. This time Grandpa caught him as he sprang forward, and the sound of his fist in Rip's face crackled. Rip slid on the floor, knocking over a spitoon. But he got up, blood dripping from his hateful mouth, and charged in again.

Twice Rip's great clublike fists caught Grandpa and knocked him across the room; however, they were glancing blows and their damage was minimal. Repeatedly, Grandpa avoided Rip's blind assaults and drove his fists into the distorted and bloody face, but still the enraged bully rushed in. Onlookers called upon Rip to give up, but he did not hear them. Finally Rip was knocked almost on top of the pool table and came up brandishing a cue stick. Grandpa attacked with a series of savage blows, and at last Rip uttered a low moan and sank senseless to the floor.

Someone gave him a cursory examination, propped him into a chair, and drinks were ordered up for Grandpa! Trembling, I came from beneath the pool table. Grandpa looked at me, laughed, and said, "Boy, what the devil were you doing under that table?"

I murmured something about trying to stay out of the way.

"I thought for a while I was gonna' need your help," he said.

Turning to the crowd at the bar, Grandpa said, "Gentlemen, I thank you for the drinks, they'll ease the pain in my hand." He suspected he had broken a small bone, and indeed, he had.

On the way home Grandpa turned and regarded me quizzically for a moment, then smiled and asked, "What are you goin' to say when we get home and they ask you what we did today?"

I hesitated a moment and said, "I'll tell them I had some strawberry pop."

"Stick to that story, boy"—he laughed—"and we'll have some more strawberry pop."

For days Grandpa nursed his tumescent hand and muttered something about getting it caught in the double trees while unhitching the horses. In the barn I saw him vigorously applying horse liniment.

The weather turned adverse in 1916. Spring brought no gentle showers, and the summer was a dreary succession of hot, cloudless days. The grain fields, normally great billowing rectangles, were reduced to scraggy patches, incapable of hiding the sunbaked ground.

The harvest was poor, but the spirits of Dad and Mother were high. Next year would be different and all would be well.

The rain did return in 1917. The land responded with its old generosity. The grain fields again were deep green seas, and boisterous laughter came back to the ranch houses. The grass on the prairie grew lush, and the cattle, gorging themselves on the rich pasturage, filled out their gaunt winter hollows.

Grandpa, playing a hunch, had planted about seventy-five acres to flax, which was commanding a fantastic price on the fitful grain market. I can recall going with him to the edge of the flax field and watching as he threw his hat into the waving grain. His hat would settle on top and ride there, so thick and strong was the growth. The wheat too was a certain thirty-five-bushel-per-acre crop!

Then out of the west, ruin thundered in on a tremendous white cloud, fringed and streaked with black. The wind suddenly abated. There was a hush, and the prairie awaited the oncoming violence. It came with the roar of a hundred express trains and seized the landscape in a frightening, pounding, savage barrage of ice.

The hailstorm lasted no more than a minute or a minute and a half. They are always brief and decisive. The white cloud rode on to the east, scattering its load of destruction over the prairie.

Grandpa put on his hat, left the house and walked toward the flax field. I trudged silently at his side. Where the grains had waved and billowed in the wind only ten minutes before, now it was difficult to detect that the fields had borne a crop. A few stems stuck forlornly from the pulverized ground, but that was all. The labor of another year was wiped out; the high hope and expectation were obliterated. Grandpa reached down and picked up a clod of the black, wet soil. Slowly he crumbled it and let it fall from his hand. When we returned to the house, Mother averted her head lest she reveal the tears.

It was the succeeding year that nature displayed still another of her willful and calamitous phenomena. The crop was only of modest proportion and promise, but it was all we had. It would have been sufficient to carry us through the coming winter; to be sure, in something less than the grand style.

This time the cloud came wheeling and twisting out of the east, and it was black and menacing. Suddenly it blotted out the sun, and the world was filled with a dreadful host of flying, buzzing, crawling, insects. They rained against the east walls of the buildings and fell into writhing drifts on the ground. They drove like bullets into the face. The livestock, in desperation, ran in from the pasture and sought protection in the barns and sheds. The ground was a boiling mass of locusts.

All that day, the infestation gripped the land. Night came, with the myriad pests beating against the walls and windows. In defeat and despair we went to bed. Another year had vanished through the crunching mandibles and labia of the locusts.

Next morning the tragedy was playing out. The cloud of winged destruction was rising and moving on to the west, leaving the ground littered with those which had perished. The fields were a pitiful waste-land of skeletal stalks and stems. Some of the more slender fence posts had been eaten off at the base, and the larger ones wore a deep indentation. Corners of buildings at ground level and the stout boards on the corral were beveled along the edges.

Only Grandma's turkeys profited from the sickening and ghastly tragedy. They walked about in exaltation, stuffing their craws to the bursting point with the inexplicable harvest of live feed.

These sudden disasters were only more dramatic

than the drought which seared and burned the great prairie. Its fingers touched slow death onto the fields and grassland, crept up the sides of the coulees and clutched at the hilltops. It stifled the wheat stems, throttled the spikes, curled the long slender leaves and bordered their edges with yellow.

The days were a dreary succession of sameness which grew into weeks, and the days and the weeks bore down on the courage of those who worked and loved the land. The great white clouds towered up from the west, high as a man's despair. Sometimes they had black fringes, and as they rolled over the land they would hurl a few scattered drops of rain at the parched earth. The big drops clattered as they struck the dry leaves of the grain, and they raised a little puff of dust where they hit the ground. The soil was baked into myriad sizes and fanciful shapes of thin crust, raised and curled at the edges.

The lake at the southern extremity of the ranch dried up completely, and I wandered across its desolate bed, picking up small shells and the bleaching bones of great frogs and water beetles. The Indians said that never in the memory of their fathers and their grandfathers had the lake been dry.

And the face of the prairie changed, perhaps forever. The incredible grass disappeared without a sign or token that it had once billowed from horizon to horizon in endless, unlimited abundance. It was, I am certain, the prime fault of Mother Nature. Without the spring and summer showers and with little snow crop in the wintertime, the roots of the miraculous buffalo grass were impaired or perhaps killed. To be sure, the pasture lands and the open ranges had been grazed, but not that intensively. It may have been the combination of the drought and the grazing that caused the grass to disappear. Its place was taken by a shorter and much more sparse variety.

We were now engaged in a brutal and soul-crushing struggle for survival. We came to know the stark face of poverty and avoided dire want only by unceasing toil and the fierce pride of my parents and grandparents. Several of the prairie families had "gone on relief," and I can remember some talk about it in tones to indicate that it was the supreme disaster which could overtake an individual or a family.

The population of the prairie communities began to dwindle. Here and there stood an empty house looking out on weed-grown fields. The long drought began to claim its victims.

Grandpa and Dad were forced to revise their planning to cope with the grim, destructive tantrum of nature. They would have to wait out the drought and spate of disasters by depending upon the livestock to pull them through to the time when there would be harvests again. They decided to break a few more acres of sod and plant it to alfalfa for winter feed. If the winters were sufficiently mild, the cattle could graze off the pasture land and nearby sections of open range, and the alfalfa would tide them over to spring. The one basic cash crop would be cream from the small herd of about a dozen cows. The weekly cream check from the creamery in town would be augmented by sale of the annual crop of young steers.

Grandpa also managed to acquire a small band of sheep by running a herd for a season and taking his pay in ewes. Some of the surrounding coulees and buttes were ideal for sheep-grazing.

But nature had other cruel surprises in store. For at least two of the remaining years, rust attacked the grain crops and sharply reduced the yield. Just as the grain was beginning to turn from green to yellow in the fields, the first faint signs of the rust-colored spores appeared on the stems and heads. From the soft kernels of grain, the microscopic spores stole the vitality and substance, leaving only a husk and a shell.

It would be a decade before the land-grant state colleges of the Northwest would discover that the key to the life cycle of the rust spore was the Japanese barberry bush, which unsuspecting farmers had purchased and planted for landscaping around their homes. In the thirties, corps of college students traveled through the Northwest, destroying every barberry bush, which acted as a winter host for the rust spore. That ended the plague.

It was about 1917 or 1918 that the Russian thistle first appeared on the prairie. It probably spread and propagated as the native buffalo grass declined, for without the grass there was little to impede the thistle from tumbling across the land, sowing its millions of microscopic seeds. Some said it had entered the country with sample shipments of new wheat seed from czarist Russia. Whatever its source, the hardy, indestructible weed had taken command of the prairie within two or three years. It choked out the grain, it thrived on drought. It broke loose from its flimsy roots in the early fall to bounce and tumble across the land and reseed itself, then it piled up in great mountainous drifts against the fences, stretching the wire and breaking fence posts.

In desperation, Grandpa and Dad resolved to try the Russian thistle as a source of energy for the livestock. If the thistle insisted on taking over the land, perhaps it could be used to some advantage. When the crop of thistles was still green and before its spikes had hardened and become brittle, it was cut—then raked in windrows and stacked like hay to keep the inside of the great mound green and moist.

The snow settled over the winter prairie, and the livestock, unable to find grass, had to be brought in for feeding. Grandpa and Dad dug into the stack of thistle and scattered it on the white snow near the hungry animals. They lowered their great heads, sniffed at the strange feed and hesitantly tasted it. One beautiful young Hereford bull, whom I had reared on skimmed milk, petted and christened "Billy," thoughtfully chewed on his mouthful of thistle, looked balefully at us, then turned his head and stared out across the snow-covered land. Neither there nor in front of him on the ground was there nourishment. It was obvious that the cattle would eat Russian thistle only if they were on the brink of starvation, and it was equally clear that the weed was virtually devoid of food value.

Fortunately, the weather cleared in a few days, and a chinook wind removed the snow cover.

The chinook is one of those phenomena of Montana weather . . . nature's remorseful caress following in due course one of her violent fits. It is an unheralded and sudden warm, dry wind, gentle as a Caribbean zephyr, sliding silently down the eastern slopes of the wintered Rockies, shrinking the great snowpacks. Because of its relatively low moisture content, Montana's land does not freeze into an impenetrable, solid mass. There are few, if any, autumnal rains. Indian summer is ended with snow flurries. Thus the melting snow drips down through its white blanket and enters the earth, creating no flood hazards, preparing the soil for its springtime exertion, and checking the risk of devastating runoff in April. Many times I have watched a great snowdrift outside the window gradually shrivel and disappear in the balmy envelopment of the chinook.

The livestock engaged in the grim contest between their reserves of fat tissue and arrival of April, when the pastures and range would produce their new growth. Hides hung loosely over their exposed ribs, and gaunt hollows developed in front of their hips.

Dad ruefully measured the sacks of potatoes in the root cellar and guessed that we had a few more than we might require to see us through the winter. The pitiful surplus was spread out in the corral, and the cattle were herded in. Eagerly, they consumed the potatoes. The next morning they were let out to forage for what little grass they might find in the frozen pasture. One splendid cow remained near the corral. Suddenly she wheeled and began to run in a circle, round and round, the circle getting smaller. Before Dad could reach her, she stopped abruptly and fell to the ground —dead! An autopsy revealed that she had choked to death on a potato!

Drought, locusts, rust, Russian thistle, hail and assorted reversals had depleted not only our capital but the spirit of my parents and grandparents. It became necessary to start looking for ways to escape the insatiable drain on their resources—financial and psychological. There were bills to be paid in town. They must be settled; that was a point of honor and conscience. The federal government's seed-loan program was about all that permitted sufficient wherewithal to get a new crop of seed into the ground each spring. The few steers sent to market or sold in town brought paltry prices. At the end of the war the wool market weakened, and lambs brought prices so low that Grandpa's venture with the sheep was barely profitable. The faithful cows and constant yield of cream were all that interceded between us and actual want.

But it was many years before I knew or realized that we had been virtually poverty-stricken. The courage of my parents was monumental. I never heard a word of self-pity as the wheels of the weather gods ground at their spirits. We were healthy, there was always enough to eat, and more to do. We had our simple pleasures.

Through the ranch years Dad maintained his "license" as a railroad telegrapher. Once in a while the Great Northern would be in desperate need of a temporary telegrapher to fill in for a regular employee who was ill. Consequently, Dad could usually secure "passes" or free railroad transportation for the family.

I was six years old that winter when, following a good harvest, Dad and Mother decided we would spend the severe-weather months in southern Missouri, visiting Grandpa and Grandma. They had gone there a few months earlier to dispose of a farm which Grandma's father had willed to her. Dad and Mother speculated mildly on the possibility of selling the Montana ranch and relocating on the Missouri property.

The ranch was left in the care of a well-recommended fellow, and we journeyed off to Missouri for several months. I can recall very little about this brief interlude beyond Wadine and me tramping to the little rural dry-goods store, the gathering of black walnuts in the woods, and the severe weather which kept us confined to the house. The return to the ranch, however, was vivid.

I was at that age when the bond between boy and dog is enduring. Shep would have explored the Missouri woods and chased the red squirrels, but he would be waiting at the ranch. The caretaker dutifully met us in Saco, and it seemed that Dad and Mother were perpetrating a needless and altogether frivolous delay when they decided to have lunch in town before driving home. Why had the caretaker failed to bring Shep into town? He would always stay with the team of horses whether they were put up in the livery stable or hitched on the street. Seated at the restaurant table, I impatiently restrained the questions concerning Shep until all the talk of livestock and weather and feed had been exhausted. Unable to wait longer, I asked how my dog was.

As casually and heartlessly as if he were announcing the death of a chicken, the caretaker answered, "Oh yeah, the dog . . . he got killed somehow . . . found him up there on the west pasture."

I turned away and rested my head on the back of the chair . . . sick and numb. Homecoming had degenerated into revolting despair. If we had never left, it could not have happened.

And indeed it would not have. We learned later that the caretaker had set out scores of coyote traps and had taken no precaution against Shep's tripping them. He had found Shep in one of the traps, his leg broken, and had shot my dog with his rifle.

Mother's chief concern about the welfare of us children on the ranch was her desperate fear of rattlesnakes. Shep had been a staunch guardian, thrusting Wadine or me aside, barking strenuously for help, frightening the snake away; and several times he had seized the reptile safely behind the head and dispatched it.

Something forever vanished from the ranch when Shep failed to come bounding down the lane to greet us.

One wintry morning, when the windows bore an inch of frosty jungle drawings, Mother cautioned me to bundle up particularly well. A stocking cap was pulled low over my ears and forehead, and a woolen scarf was tied securely over my mouth and nose, forcing me to breathe through it. Mother warned me to go no farther than the barn and then come back in a few minutes, check the thermometer on the outside of the house and let her know what it read.

I stepped outside into a strange eeriness. The snow crackled underfoot like shots of a cap pistol. My breath coming through the folds of the scarf created a cloud which hung in the air. I walked a few steps toward the barn and glanced back at the house. From the chimney arose a thin column of smoke that ascended up and up in a straight, clean line. I heard shouts and conversation and realized that I was overhearing the Osiers and the Pinkermans as they worked at their morning chores more than a mile distant. The air was sheer crystal, and tiny fragments of frost danced in it. The livestock were ringed tightly about the strawstack, their heads and shoulders buried deep within its protection.

I raced once around the barn, gathered an egg or two from the reluctant hens and ran back toward the house. On the porch I stood on tiptoe to read the thermometer. Seventy-six degrees below zero!

No one remained outside for any length of time that day. As night approached, it grew a little warmer, and by the next day the thermometer was back at a modest 40 below.

Inside, we were comfortable and warm. On the coldest days we dipped into the precious supply of coal, but otherwise most of our heat came from the cow chips.

The evenings were delightful. The family sat about a huge round table over which hung a splendid lamp— an old Coleman gasoline burner, antecedent of the Coleman lantern. Its mesh mantles burned white-hot, and it had to be pumped up. Boasting a great white shade and an attractive handle, by which it could be suspended from the ceiling, it threw off a magnificent white light, hissing contentedly and filling the room with a clean odor.

I have frequently thought of trying to find an old Coleman lamp to hang in my home or office, but I shudder to think what it might do to building inspectors and insurance rates.

About the table Mother and Grandma worked on the pile of mending, or they crocheted and knitted. Grandpa was buried within his newspaper, usually the Kansas City *Star*, which arrived almost a week late. Our mail was now delivered once a week and placed in the mailbox on the ranch gate. Previously we had picked it up in town. Grandpa insisted on the *Star* because it kept him informed of his beloved Kansas City, and its thorough, unyielding Republicanism measured up to his specifications. Dad was usually engrossed in a book. During the war years, I pored over the maps, drawings, cartoons, accounts and pictures of the action in France, and drew pictures of Germans with spiked helmets.

Under the rays of the friendly lamp, Mother worked with me and taught me to "sound out the letters" and put the words together. I scrawled letters to my uncle who was "somewhere in France."

Mother sent to "Monkey" Ward's for several games. On the big table we played Rook and Old Maid and Authors, while the wind howled outside and blew the icy snow particles against the windows. Frequently, Grandma would enter from the kitchen with a heaping bowl of buttered popcorn or a platter of homemade candy. Wadine would sit patiently while Mother or Grandma lavished time and affection on the care of her long blond curls.

On those sub-zero winter nights, the delicate business of going to the toilet on the side of the hill behind the house was something to delay as long as possible. There was certainly no idling in our "bathroom," and no one, in wintertime at least, ever inquired of another if he intended "to stay in there all day." In our family, somehow, the word for body waste came to be "Oh-oh." I have a suspicion it derived from the involuntary expletive when one sat down on that frost-covered seat! In this respect, we males enjoyed a distinct advantage over the opposite sex.

Many winter nights the mysterious gods of the far north put on spectacular displays. The aurora borealis, immense and silent, sent its streamers and shafts of colored light from horizon to zenith. It frequently began with only a great blue-white curtain of light hanging delicately from the northern sky. Then the curtain would rip asunder and explode into fountains, cascades and giant globules of rose, blue-violet, green and amber. One rarely spoke while the northern lights were dancing, for such an incredible show seemed to justify sound. It demanded gigantic peals and waves of overwhelming accompaniment, but it was silent and intimidated into silence anything which might not match its proportions.

Dad now began to return to railroading, but still on a part-time basis, working what was called the "second trick," from four in the afternoon until midnight, seven days a week. He invested in an automobile . . . one of Henry Ford's earlier models. Whatever its capricious character, and it had that in generous measure, it carried Dad back and forth, daily, from ranch to town. The check from the Great Northern, twice per month, was more money than my parents had seen in several years!

In August, a series of heavy thunderstorms boiled up out of the west. We had become accustomed to prairie storms, but these were of a nature so violent that Wadine and I went to bed each evening fearful that we would be awakened again by the ear-shattering, deafening bombardment. Every night, for a week, carrying no rain, the storms crashed down upon us. The mornings, invariably, were clear and bright.

It was the last in the cycle of storms, and it descended upon the ranch with an earth-quaking roar about one o'clock in the morning. We were obviously in the very center of it, for there was no time lapse between the blinding, blue-white, crackling flashes of lightning and the horrifying claps of thunder. The windows threatened to implode; the house felt as though it were being picked up and shaken.

I was lying in my bed, staring in fright at the ceiling. Suddenly, I heard the terrified neighing of one of the horses. I dashed to the window and saw a jagged line of fire cleaving the barn from the ground, up the side, over the roof, and down the other side. Flames were licking at both edges of the gash which the lightning had cut through the building. Pandemonium had seized the area around and near the burning barn. Sheep were running about inside the corral. Chickens were cackling, several horses inside the barn were neighing in terror.

Dad was on his way home from a day at the depot in town. As his Ford reached the elevation looking down into our basin, he saw the flames! At that distance he could not determine whether it was the house or one of the outbuildings which was on fire. In the darkness, aided only by the weak lights which flickered on the front of the car, he raced toward the ranch. Dad reached the barn at the same moment as Grandpa and the rest of us. I responded to Grandpa's shouted com-

mand and opened the corral to let out the frightened
sheep. Grandpa and Dad rushed into the burning barn,
threw halter ropes about the necks of the horses and
led them to safety. The cows in the adjoining barn
were herded out by Mother, and Grandma was rescu-
ing her precious chickens, turkeys, and my geese. One
hen with a brood of young chicks refused to be shooed
out of the barn, where she had elected to nest in the
hay stanchion. She was unable to gather her confused
and frightened little flock, and the last we saw of her
she was trying to gather them together and lead them
to safety in her own way.

With the rescue work completed, there was nothing
to do but watch the barn burn to the ground. The
lightning storm had brought with it no rain, and the
flames soon reduced the structure to a skeleton of burning studs and beams. Dad and Grandpa concentrated
on the adjoining cowshed and were able to save it, but
Grandma's chicken house went with the barn.

This latest in the long succession of disasters and
rural tragedies was neither decisive nor ultimate. In
terms of dollars and cents it was by no means as disastrous as the loss of a crop, but it was perhaps a final
psychological blow. What else could ill luck devise? It
was as if nature and circumstance, having contrived
every tested reversal and calamity, and seeing us still
hanging on stubbornly, were now resorting to just dirty
tricks. A rancher has license to question his luck when
lightning strikes and burns down his barn.

But that was the conclusion . . . the spectacular
finale . . . of the series of storms. They had rolled upon

and over us for a week, unable to frighten us off the land. In glee, the lightning danced capriciously on over the prairie, its devilish mission accomplished.

The morning came, bright and clean. The fat little grain sparrows chattered about the night's events and sought new places for shelter.

Spring was a phenomenon in Montana, and it is yet. It is an explosion of sunlight, burgeoning earth, scents, bursting buds and a sudden cessation of the raw March wind. The poignant call of the meadowlarks trills across the prairie. It is a season affecting man, animal and plant.

Spring was such a burst of energy that children were simply compelled, frequently, to jump up and down in sheer exuberance. Out on some lonely hilltop, I often filled my lungs and screamed . . . because it was spring!

The horses bucked and reared when the harness or saddle was removed following a spring day's work. The lambs played "king of the castle" on a large rock on the hillside, leaping completely over the backs of their complacent mothers. The cows sported themselves in the pasture, and the turkey gobblers almost burst their wattles in apoplectic strutting about.

My parents had provided us children with a small wagon, a scale model of the big farm wagon. One spring evening, I made out of rope a harness and slipped it innocently on Billy, the pet bull calf. He stood patiently while I hitched him to the toy wagon. Wadine and Marian were observing all these preparations and I invited them to accompany me on the first ride, and of course they leaped at the opportunity.

Marian, my second sister, sat in front, her plump little legs overhanging the wagon. Wadine sat behind her, and I was about to crowd into the back when the calf suddenly shot forward as though he had been discharged from a cannon. With the first leap, my sisters were left sitting, unhurt, on the ground. The lines snapped out of my fingers, and the calf flew around the corner of the house, bawling at the top of his lungs. A young colt, also kept in the yard, shook his head once and bolted through the small wooden gate, sending it flying in a hundred fragments. With that, one of the horses in the corral took a flying leap over the gate, caught his rear feet in it and kicked it to bits. The cows suddenly went stir-crazy inside the shed, and one emerged, bucking and bawling, with the wooden stanchion locked about her neck. Still the calf was circling the house, the toy wagon streaming out behind him as he turned the corners and banging into the sides of the house. Dad stuck his head out of the barn and shouted, "What in the name of all hell is going on?"

Mother had her head out the kitchen window, and I was rolling on the grass in hysterical laughter. My sisters were weeping in fright.

The sheep joined the bedlam and poured through the barn area, surrounding bucking horses and stampeding cows. Wire was creaking and straining, wooden gates were being smashed; and the calf continued to circumnavigate the house, with the wagon flying behind him. Grandpa and Dad frantically tried to separate sheep, lambs, colts, horses, cows, calves and squawking chickens. The whole farm had exploded into a paroxysm of suddenly released spring energy.

As quickly as it all began, it subsided, and we picked up the pieces.

Spring on the prairie inspired one to creative musings and stirrings. It was as though man, seeing and feeling this astonishing burst of life and new energy on the part of nature, responded by trying in some way to emulate her. Surely, there was, in the soul and capacity of man, something he might do to rival some of the bursting loveliness about him.

I sat in the warm sunshine on tops of the hills overlooking the ranch house, the barns, the fields and the lake bed. I lay down and put my head on the grass. I could hear it! I could hear spring! The ground was a moving, writhing, stirring mass of movement and growth. Millions of tiny shoots were probing at the warm earth, drinking its moisture, absorbing its goodness and sending their growth to the sunlight. The earth, the sky, the air, the universe were throbbing with life . . . and it was good!

Spring beckoned me to every swale, hill and coulee on the ranch and the range. I knew where the wild prairie roses grew. I brought Mother armfuls of wild sweet peas. I picked up arrowheads and moss agates. I stood on hilltops and sang . . . sang words which came to me on the spur of the moment . . . sang what I was desperately trying to say. The loveliness of earth cried out for permanence in words, in music, in paint. The world was renewing itself, and I wanted to seize upon it and hold it there, for fear it might not occur again.

The treeless prairie instilled in me, an abiding love of trees. Grandpa had brought to me, from one of his wood-gathering expeditions to Stinky Creek, a small box-elder sapling. I planted it near the well, where we could water it frequently. That small and forlorn little tree was one of my most precious treasures. I often gazed to the west at the blue outline of the Little Rockies. Dad had told me that they were blue because the atmosphere and distance turned the green of the forest to blue. I imagined myself wandering over the slopes of the mountain range in the cool shade of the trees.

The Milk River, to me, was a constant fairyland, because of its trees. I longed to climb every one of them to the very top, to know every branch and twig.

In the farthest coulee at the northwest corner of the ranch I had found a small ground cedar, which sufficed for a tree. My childish imagination made of it a great towering fir or redwood.

Years later I was to stand in a grove of magnificent sequoias on the headwaters of the Kern River in California and sicken as the owner of the land felled them to be cut up for fence posts. The denuded hills and mountainsides of the Northwest, where the rapacious saws and axes have taken their toll of the forests, are bitter tragedies inflicted upon all of us.

These were years of "learning by doing" . . . the ways and the care of ranch animals. As the steers approached the time for market, I moved them as little as possible, lest they lose their fatty tissue. If they were content to stand in a given area and fatten themselves, it was "money in the bank." If a calf was to be taken away from his mother and reared on skimmed milk so that the cream might be sold, it meant teaching the youngster how to drink from a bucket; and that was a task of unmitigated hell. Before the instruction was complete, patience invariably ran out, calf and instructor were soaked from head to foot in skimmed milk. The sheep always grazed into the wind to prevent flies from despositing eggs in their damp nostrils. Never approach a horse from the rear—always from the front or side—otherwise you might get the daylights kicked out of you. Watch the shoulders of the draft horses carefully, where the collars of their harnesses pulled against them; an ill-fitting collar could ruin a fine animal. Be careful when riding a saddle horse through a gate, lest he brush too closely to the post and bang your knee. When unbridling a horse, always stand to the side of his head, lest he should bolt in a bit of premature surcease from duty and run over you. When releasing horses at the end of the day, try to herd them toward some soft and grassy bit of pasture, lest, as they roll and sport themselves on the ground, they injure a shoulder on a stone and bring on a fistula.

Once in a while a young ewe encountered difficulty dropping her first lamb. When this happened I was the obstetrician because my hands and arms were small. Grandpa lathered my arm with a thick coating of soap suds. The ewe stood patiently while I probed the womb, grasped her lamb by the front feet and pulled steadily and firmly. Grandpa wisely counseled me to avoid bringing up this indelicate subject around Grandma and Mother, for that would have been the end of my obstetrical work. He always chose a place somewhere out of their sight. Even Dad, I think, looked upon the whole operation with something less than enthusiasm.

The growing lambs had to be "docked," and I learned to cut their tails, notch their ears and castrate them, quickly and deftly, and with a minimum of pain.

Occasionally, bad weather struck at lambing time. That meant picking them up the moment they dropped, wrapping them in something warm, and rushing them to the shelter of the barn or even the house.

The herding of the livestock on our own pasturage and on the open range fell, largely, to me for several reasons. I was eager to do it because it gave me the opportunity to ride a horse over the land. Moreover, I was somehow uniquely immune to mosquitoes. They drove everyone else frantic, they could swarm on a lamb and eventually kill it by consuming its blood— but I could ride or walk through dense clouds of them and come off virtually unscathed.

In a deep swale to the west of the ranch house, I noticed that the snow water collected each spring and then flowed down into the basin through a small gap in the hills, and spread out in the general area of the vegetable garden. Painfully aware of the shortage of water during those drought years, I resolved to bestow a magnificient gift upon Grandma and Mother by building a dam at the lower outlet of the swale, to provide water for the garden. I worked like a beaver on my "dam" most of that summer, during every spare moment. I tugged and perspired, digging rocks out of the surrounding hillsides and somehow transporting them to the "dam." I rolled some of them into position. With a tremendous crowbar I employed every form of leverage known to physicists, I hitched Old Bill, one of the farm horses, to the stone boat and hauled rocks on it. I threw considerable quantities of earth in between the rocks and even tamped Russian thistles into the crevices for sealing material.

Somehow, the size of my "dam" was discounted and everyone was too busy to pay any attention to the construction project of a seven-year-old boy.

Winter piled the snow on the back three-twenty, and I began to anticipate the lake which would form behind my "dam" when the spring thaw came. The weather finally turned warmer, and I was amazed at the proportions of my "lake"—it filled the entire swale and trickled over the top of the "dam." In the center, the water was possibly fifteen- or twenty-feet deep!

But my engineering was of brief duration and almost disastrous. During the night the dam gave way, sending a wall of water tumbling down the draw, through the corral, past the barn and into the garden. The next morning, the corral had a deep gorge cut through it, a corner of the barn stood several feet off the ground, and the garden looked like the delta of a river. I was reminded in stern language to leave the physical aspects of the ranch as they were and to consult some of the family elders before undertaking any more ambitious projects.

The easy and confident assumption that a horse is a sometimes unpredictable creature was one that qualified as a fundamental law of the ranch. The most ponderous old plow horse is going to have his moments.

One of my first memories is the precipitous crash to the ground from behind the saddle where Mother had placed me. The horse obviously objected to the extra bundle on his back, seated in a strange position; and he simply vaulted into the air, arched his spine, came down stiff-legged, and was rid of me.

Even steady, complacent Old Bill, a massive mixture of Clydesdale and whatever, one day thrust his mighty bulk into the air and bounced me off while I was riding him to the barn from the fields. Old Bill stood looking down at me as I lay on the ground, surprised at himself and apologetic.

My parents managed somehow to keep me dispossessed of a genuine fast horse, although that did not prevent me from riding those belonging to my friends. I was aware that should trouble develop, the wiser course suggested the extraction of feet from the stirrup, detachment from the horse in the most graceful way possible, and a fierce *hold on the reins*. It was no particular disgrace to be thrown, but to walk back home was unforgivable.

The West Bench was an inviting area over which to ride. Only the infrequent steep hillsides were rock-strewn, and a horse could be let out . . . have his head and the bit . . . in furious charges over the flat land interspersed with draws and coulees and swales. Roy Waal, Steve Osier, Danny Pinkerman and the rest of us knew the locations of the neighbors' gates, so we could traverse the Bench from Stinky Creek to the Whitewater.

My horse, Ted, was all heart and little remaining respiratory system, but his flagging resources responded to the exhilarating flow of the wind, the limitless boundaries of earth and sky, and the irresistible prospect of losing one's way in the infinite alternations of buttes, draws, coulees, swales, flats and glacial moraines. We often climbed to the crown of a high hill, from where horse and I gazed for long moments out over the wondrously malformed land. Going up or down steep inclines or traversing the outcropping of detritus, Ted was a wary adventurer. He stopped discreetly to choose his course and then proceeded in a workmanlike way. For all his ailments, he never stumbled, and for the brief distances he could manage a gallop he ran with élan: mane and tail flying, head and neck extended, feet raised high.

On the Fourth of July there was certain to be a celebration somewhere. One year it was held at the little forlorn village of Whitewater, near the border. Another time it was in Saco, but frequently it was held in the grove of trees along the Milk River.

We children began to anticipate the Fourth about the time the memories of Christmas had faded. There was the inevitable rodeo, usually a baseball game, perhaps a fabulous band which played real music in an improvised bandstand gaily decorated with bunting, and from which the congressman or the country agricultural agent delivered his Fourth of July address. There were foot races for men, women and boys; potato races, sack races and backing-up races for Model T's. Carnival entrepreneurs appeared with little booths in which the customer threw baseballs at various targets and won kewpie dolls. There were booths where rings were thrown over the heads of canes and the canes had various denominations of currency attached to them. Operators of the old shell game were there, and there were shooting galleries and early varieties of bingo. One year there was a concession in which the men threw baseballs at a target, and if they hit the bull's eye it tripped a mechanism, causing a heavily painted young woman to be thrown backward off her perch far enough to reveal her bottom for an instant. Grandma caught me observing that one and hustled me away. She almost demanded to see the man in charge of the picnic for an explanation of what that hussy was doing on the grounds. The ranch families brought huge picnic lunches and ate them in the shade of the big trees. There were refreshment stands with hot dogs, lemonade, ice cream and cotton candy for sale. I dipped into my savings to buy a few firecrackers and made a pest out of myself until they had been exploded. At night there was a fireworks display, then the grove was turned into magic as the Japanese lanterns were lit, an orchestra struck up, and the couples whirled on the improvised floor. Grandpa was the best "caller" of the square dance in the entire area, and he would send the couples through the promenade, then "gents to the inside and ladies to the out," and call for "the grand right and left." It was all so great, so grand, so noisy that a small country boy could barely endure it.

It must have been the first Fourth of July after Dad bought the car. I was up early to lend a hand with the chores, for I could not bear the thought of missing a single moment of the day's activity down on the Milk. In frustration I ran back and forth from barn to house to see how Dad was progressing with his chores and to make certain that nothing was impeding Mother and my sisters in their duties and preparations.

Ultimately, the cows were turned out to pasture, the milk was separated and the cream taken to the cellar.

Dad shaved and put on his "Sunday" suit. Mother and the girls appeared starched, scrubbed and combed. The picnic lunch was placed in the car, we all climbed in, Mother adjusted her hat, and Dad spun the crank. Nothing happened! Dad cranked again—somewhat more authoritatively. Still nothing! He cranked until the whole car bounced up and down. The black iron beast stood obstinately silent in its tracks.

Dad leaned into the front-seat section, switched the magneto off and on, adjusted the spark and gas levers and cranked again. It was no use.

A dull, sickening knot of anxiety was gathering in my stomach. What if the car refused to start? If we had to go to the celebration in the wagon, it would be hours before we could get there! I had visions of missing the Montana cowboy champion riding Sunfish in the rodeo.

Dad placed his hat on the front seat and spun the crank some more. Sweat stood out on his forehead and dripped from his chin. He leaned on the front of the car, panting, and cussed quietly at the shiny brass radiator. Mother cautioned us to sit still and say nothing. She looked about innocently and serenely as though the lovely scenery were flying past. My eyes were fixed on Dad. "Don't give up! Surely, somehow, it will start! Give it another try, Dad!"

Dad raised the hood and peered inside. He cranked the monster again, but to no avail.

Quietly, Mother gathered the girls, and they tiptoed out of the car and into the house. I had raised the front seat and taken out the jack.

Dad hoisted one rear wheel into the air, put the car in gear and spun the crank again. It rocked on its perch, the wheel spun, but the engine never so much as coughed. It was the most lifeless, inarticulate and inert assembly of iron that had ever tried the patience of man; and it was about to break the heart of a small boy.

Dad asked me to see how quickly I could get a team in from the pasture. On the verge of tears, I was off like a shot. In a half-hour or so, we had a team harnessed and hitched to the Ford. Mother had discreetly appeared in case her help was required. Dad did not need to tell me to urge the team into a run, for I was all too aware that this was the last chance of getting the car started. If it failed to respond to a boost from the horses, our Fourth was going to be spent right there at home and we would eat our magnificent lunch in the shade of the house.

Dad adjusted levers, grasped the wheel, and nodded. I shouted at the team and cracked Old Bill on his ample behind with the end of a line. We made a big circle and headed down the lane toward the ranch gate. Dad suddenly stepped on the clutch and threw the Ford into low gear. The wheel skidded for a sickening moment, took hold, and the engine burst into a mighty roar, the fenders shivering and vibrating!

I quickly unhitched the horses, ran them to the barn; we removed their harnesses and turned them back to pasture. The Ford was clattering merrily at the yard gate. Mother and the girls were sitting primly in the back seat once again. Dad stepped on the clutch, and we bounced jauntily down the dusty lane.

Vying with Christmas and the Fourth of July was the annual harvest. It was a time of intense excitement, a great influx of people, neighborliness, mountains of delicious food, and (if the crop was good) a period of general conviviality and good cheer.

The green of the grain fields began to pale, and a definite shade of bright gold took its place. The heads of the wheat stalks developed long beards, and the oats hung heavily on their stems.

Prelude to the harvest was overhaul of the big binder, the largest piece of machinery on the land, replaced today by the more gigantic combines. The sickles were sharpened, the canvas conveyors mended, the binding and tying mechanisms checked. Binding twine, in large heavy rolls, was brought from town.

Then one morning, Dad or Grandpa entered the field with the binder, Wadine and I trooping behind. The great machine bit into the field on its initial swath. The sickles whirred, the great windlass began to turn, its blades catching the grain stalks and bending them into the cutter. Precisely and evenly the stalks fell onto the canvas conveyor, and they were lifted up to disappear into the maw of the binder. There was a clank and a clatter of gears and iron against iron as the first bundle or ripe grain was ejected and rolled into the swath just cut. Wadine and I tugged at the bundles, trying to help Dad or Grandpa set them into shocks. The size and value of the crop was quickly apparent by the frequency with which the bundles rolled from the binder. The grain remained in the shock to protect it from rain and dew until the thresher arrived.

This was the climax of the harvest. Over the rim of the basin and up the road came the great black steam engine, pulling the giant separator behind it. Following the separator were the neighbors in their hayracks to help us harvest. The neighbors' wives had arrived earlier with their cakes and pies and assorted casseroles.

The engine shrilled a blast from its whistle as it turned in our gate and clanked up the lane, sending occasional jets of black smoke into the sky. Wadine and I raced a half mile to meet it, and the engineer stopped and lifted us into the cab.

As we neared the house, Dad or Grandpa indicated where the strawstack was to be and the separator was placed accordingly. The engine was unhooked and set at a distance about seventy-five feet away. The great belt was unwound from its rack and slipped onto the flywheels of engine and separator. Three blasts from the whistle told the field crew and teamsters that the engine crew was ready—bring in the first load.

The wagons, their broad racks piled high, drew up close to the gaping mouth of the great machine. Its canvas conveyor was like the giant tongue of some primordial beast, and it fed the bundles to a bank of revolving knives . . . the slashing teeth and fangs. The bundles tumbled into the maw, and we watched, fascinated, for the first blast of chaff and straw from the blower pipe. There was a moment's pause, the separator whirred from within its cavernous insides, and then a puff of dust and chaff shot from the mouth of the pipe and settled on the ground. We ran around to the other side to see the first bushel of grain flow from the chute into the wagon.

If the threshing required more than one day, the neighbors went back to their own ranches for the night, but the engine and separator crewmen unrolled their beds on the ground or slept in the hayloft.

The harvest meals were shameless competitions of abundance. Each ranch wife was a keen competitor for the ultimate decision of the threshing crew that she had served the finest food of the season. I am not certain about the justice of their decisions, but it guaranteed them a perpetuating array of food. Chicken was the standard meat dish, but occasionally lamb or even beef was served. The variety of vegetables included everything the gardens could produce. There were side dishes of macaroni or spaghetti, dried beans, hominy, stewed tomatoes, pickles. The dessert department was like the cake-and-pie booth of a county fair. Each farm wife had brought her best, and she had devious ways of letting it be known which was hers.

Even as the harvest was over and the machinery was pulled away, there was yet the new strawstack to climb, tunnel under and explore.

In the vicinity of the barnyard grew a fantastic weed which we called "lamb's quarter." Its tender leaves when young made splendid greens, but by late summer it had grown six or seven feet tall, and through this forest of lamb's quarter, Wadine and I played our imaginative games.

It appeared that the ground rules and the objective of our game were somewhat ambiguous, and a considerable portion of the play was given to earnest discussion of how the rules might be refined and codified. There was a "good guy" and a "bad guy," naturally; and again, naturally, I was consistently the "good guy." Wadine not only had a constantly villainous role, but she had a durable name . . . "Joe Harper." Years later she was to tell me that she had frequently become "darned sick and tired of Joe Harper," and that she had longed to play the heroic role just once! The patch of lamb's quarter was the scene of many violent and tense confrontations with the hopelessly antisocial and irascible outcast, but truth, honesty, and virtue always prevailed—until Wadine wearied of Joe Harper and walked into the house.

Rarely has a small boy been blessed with a smaller sister of such character . . . with such a capacity for patience and affection. Wadine was taciturn, a marvelous listener, and she is yet. She would listen gravely, by the hour, to my fanciful boastings and declarations of astounding intent. Wadine solemnly agreed . . . or permitted me to believe she agreed . . . that I would, indeed, ride the stallion right into Saco! I would one day shoot and bring home over my heroic shoulders the carcass of a gray wolf! I would learn to swim and I could run faster than the wind! I could throw and pin Roy Waal with one hand tied behind me and I was not afraid to ride Billy, the Hereford bull! Childish secrets were safe with Wadine. She did not tell our parents when I tried to smoke a stalk of lamb's quarter.

One day, at play, I had been much too rough with Wadine, and Mother seized from the closet the ultimate weapon: the willow switch. With what swelling surge of affection I have recalled over the years how Wadine's eyes gushed with tears as she beseeched Mother to spare me the terrible punishment.

Her "no-nonsense" and steady character were illustrated the day I fell out of the barn loft. Wadine surmises that she may have pushed me, but I doubt it. In any event as we jostled on the brink of the hay trap, I suddenly plummeted through the opening and crashed onto the floor of the barn. As Mother tells the story, Wadine calmly and with magnificent insouciance entered the house and suggested that "Someone should see what is wrong with that boy out there. He can't talk." It must have resulted in a mild concussion, for I had no recollection of the remainder of that day or that evening.

Once in town, when I was engaged in a fight with a

schoolmate and I was being badly outpointed, I recall Wadine standing by and sobbing.

It was spring; the time for promises and when nature said "I'm sorry." Dad and I were wandering around the lake, checking on a herd of steers which grazed on the thick grass along the shore.

Suddenly an explosion of wings erupted under my horse's feet, and with a series of honks, a wild Canadian goose took wing and flew off over the lake.

Dad and I dismounted, and found beneath the ledge of an overhanging rock at the water's edge a nest containing four large eggs. On rare occasions the wild waterfowl would nest on the infrequent bodies of water in northern Montana. They were either the unorthodox and wayward members of the flights, or they somehow deduced that the long air journey on into Canada made little sense, when there were nesting facilities to the south.

On our knees beside the nest Dad and I conceived the notion of taking the eggs back to the ranch house and putting them under a hen. Carefully we placed the eggs in our hats and rode off.

A benevolent and unsuspecting old hen was only too pleased as we tucked the large eggs beneath her. She ruffled her feathers contentedly, wiggled her plump body and settled down to her patient vigil. Each morning I checked the undercarriage of the hen, for we had no notion how near the eggs might be to their hatching period. Four or five days went by.

But one morning I ran from the chicken house with a triumphant shout. The eggs had hatched, and beneath the old biddy were four squirming, down-covered baby geese!

Poor old hen—What a problem those children were. Baby chicks are born with the ability to pick their food from the ground, but not geese. They are, like most other birds, dependent upon the parent to stuff the food down their gullets. The hen clucked herself into a neurosis, trying to instruct her four strange offspring into picking their food from the ground, but they stood around her, chirping and squeaking, their heads stuck in the air and their tiny mouths agape. In desperation I tried stuffing them with worms and bread crumbs, but a small bird requires an amazing quantity of food. It was clear that the lives of the four young geese depended on how quickly they might learn to forage.

Environment and stimulus ultimately conquered inherent characteristic—the young geese began to eat from the ground. Their rate of growth was astonishing.

The old hen called and clucked to them at sundown each night, and they responded. She settled herself on the floor of the chicken house, spread her wings, fluffed out her feathers and tried desperately to brood her impossible charges. However, within a few days they were almost as large as she. What a sight! The poor old biddy strained to make herself as large and accom-

modating as possible, but great portions of her youngsters remained exposed no matter what she did. One of
the young geese would shift his position beneath her,
and the confused hen would find herself teetering precariously on the strong back of her child.

They were soon capable of shifting completely for
themselves, and the frustrated foster mother was glad
to be rid of them.

Summer passed and the four geese had grown into
magnificent birds. They waddled to the water trough
and splashed about in it, they roamed across the pasture land, foraging for grasshoppers and beetles; but in
a solemn and dignified parade, one behind the other,
they returned to the protection of the chicken house at
evening.

They were incredible guards and protectors. If a
team and rig or car turned in at the ranch gate a half
mile away, the four geese set up a wild cacaphony of
honking and hissing. They would stand in a compact
grouping, their heads high, their beautiful white chests
thrust forward toward the offending interloper. At
night, occasionally, they awakened the entire ranch
from within their shelter, and we knew that a coyote or
some other animal was prowling about.

One evening I made the error of trying to hurry
them into the chicken house. They were not to be hurried and I was a menace to their dignity! The leader of
the column suddenly turned on me, hissed angrily from
his open beak, threw out his chest, and clouted me on
the side of the head with one of his wings. I had been
kicked by horses and cows, but I had never been hit

that hard. I picked myself up with a new respect for my prizes.

Autumn came a few days sooner than we expected. The four geese were parading back toward the barnyard, when suddenly they halted and stretched their long necks to the sky. High overhead an early flight was racing southward in perfect V formation with one guard protecting the squadron wing. My geese hesitated a moment. They shifted their weight from one foot to the other. Their wings involuntarily trembled and shuddered. Then, with a cry, they ran a few steps and arose on wing.

I stood there, awe-stricken. We had intended to clip their wings, but that early flight had taken us by surprise.

My four birds gained altitude, flew over the barnyard and house, honking at the geese which were disappearing. They flew in pursuit and became four small specks against the sky. I turned to go to the house and report what had happened. But as I reached the door, I heard their honking! From the south, at low level, my geese were returning. They had been unable to overtake their fellows and they had turned back to the comfort of their chicken house. They landed below the corral, easily and gracefully, shook the strain out of their wings and marched majestically into the barnyard.

The next morning we clipped the long feathers on their wings. As the succeeding flights went overhead, honking and calling, frustration and indecision frequently seized the four birds. Occasionally, they tried to lift off, but their clipped wings no longer caught the air. The moment the flight had passed, their poise returned.

One evening only three of the geese came back to the barnyard and their behavior indicated that something was amiss. I herded them into their roost, and in the gathering dusk, ran toward the well and the area where they had been grazing. I searched the hillside and the pasture below. Presently I saw it: a scattering of white feathers on the grass. The ground had been disturbed, and there were splashes of blood on the stones and grass blades along a route leading up the hillside. I ran to the top and peered into the semidarkness, but I could see nothing. It was obvious that a coyote had cleverly tracked his quarry and dashed in quickly to take the geese by surprise.

But the following morning, in the barnyard, stood our heroic and wounded bird! Half his feathers were torn off, and the abrasions and cuts were ugly. One wing was damaged and his head was a mass of congealed blood.

However, he had made his way home in triumph, conquering a coyote in a savage encounter of beak and wing against fang. The generous protective covering of feathers had obviously prevented the coyote from securing his death grip, and the great powerful wings had beaten off the interloper. The goose responded to care, and soon he was well.

A year later, Dad and Mother reluctantly decided that one of the great olive-green and white birds would grace our Thanksgiving table. With grim resolve he carried the noble creature to the woodpile and draped the long graceful neck over the chopping block. For whatever reason, the trusting bird offered little protest and submitted to his impending fate with an air of utter resignation. The cruel ax rose and then remained poised. The three other honkers burst into wild bugling and hissing. Propelling themselves with their wings, they skittered across the barnyard and set upon the executioner. In relieved defeat, my father released the creature, and happily rewarded the show of mutual defense which our four charges had displayed in response to some strange signal of danger to one.

Several years later, when we left the ranch, the geese were sold to a neighbor on the Whitewater, where, hopefully, they might breed with a group which he had raised under similar circumstances. I never learned whether the experiment was successful, but I would doubt it. While the first generation might adapt itself to domesticity with apparent ease, yet there was a constant struggle between the wild and the tamed manifest in their behavior. When the haunting call of the migratory periods was suppressed in those finely tuned and sensitive creatures, it is quite likely that the mating instinct was disrupted too.

Somewhere, at some vague point in those innocent years, I began going to school. Although I can recall the anticipation of the momentous event, the years have somehow dimmed and all but erased any memory of the first day of a process which would occupy most of the next two decades.

One of the initial undertakings of our new outpost society was the creation of a school system. A school district was created in conformity with the laws and requirements of the state, and the settlers, in duly constituted and recorded assembly, elected a school board and assessed themselves to provide for the construction of a schoolhouse and the hiring of a teacher. It appeared that our land, lying approximately halfway between Stinky Creek and Whitewater, was selected as the ideal site. Consequently, Dad set aside an acre in the extreme northeast corner of our half-section, and the little rectangular one-room schoolhouse, with its row of windowpanes facing southward, and two privies out behind, became known as "the Huntley school."

A generous and deserving woman's club in Saco has long since moved the little building into town, restored it, supplied it with snapshots and photographs of its early clientele, and otherwise preserved it as a reminder of the community's rough-hewn, frontier past.

Our "little white schoolhouse" must be awed and self-consciously out of place in town, among other buildings. It has lost its air of loneliness. It represents no more the hope and confidence of better days to come, but is a monument to human defeat . . . to the immutable and tenacious invincibility of the grassland. The windowpanes, like sad eyes, no longer look out over the West Bench and weep. The simple little

schoolhouse, however, has been rescued from the ig-
nominious fate of all the other ranch buildings of the
area—which simply vanished and turned the horizon
of the benchland back to its unbroken union of land
and sky.

The schoolhouse, in addition to its prime function,
served as the community center. There were nights
when it cast a warm glow into the pasture and down
the lane. The old piano thumped merrily, and the fid-
dle shrilled its sprightly tunes. The rural wives were
whirled about the floor, and the men might repair occasionally to the row of teams and rigs hitched outside
for cautious nips at a bit of bottled "spirit."

The schoolhouse was occasionally converted to a
"house of the Lord," on Sundays when the Methodist
"sky pilot" from town was moved to visit our area or
when some itinerant missionary or evangelist might
appear. And the county agent, too, conducted infrequent meetings in the schoolhouse. I recall one evening
meeting at which he applauded my father and grandfather for deemphasizing farming in behalf of cash
grain crops to utilize the land for livestock instead.
There ensued a general discussion concerning the use
of the unclaimed land and cooperative ownership and
use of herd bulls.

The auction-supper was the most tried-and-sure
method of raising funds for the school or for any other
civic project. Each farm wife or eligible daughter prepared a "supper" for two, packed it, wrapped it in the
fanciest paper and decoration available, and brought it
to the party. After a few hours of dancing, the boxes

were sold at auction. The highest bidder for each package received not only the contents but the companionship of the housewife who had prepared it. The auction process was invariably an occasion for good-natured jibing and joking.

The schoolhouse was also the setting for funerals, for christenings, for marriages, and elections. It was, indeed, a community center, in that it housed the collective joys and sorrows of the neighborhood. It administered to the young, it was drafted into service in behalf of the souls and the fortunes of the adults, and it was a temple for the last rites of the aged. Before it was endowed with the distinction of an historical landmark and packed into town, it accrued an aura of stubborn permanency, standing there on its little knoll, by the lane, a quarter mile south of Osier's, for fifty years or more. When ranch buildings of the area sank into the prairie and vanished, the little schoolhouse endured, weathering the succession of seasons, refusing to capitulate to the elements or accidents, withstanding even the vandalism which the combination of automobiles and misguided youth have set loose upon so many rural areas.

Ada Sommers, who had taught school in Wisconsin before venturing to the Montana homestead, and who had volunteered for "a turn or two," was the teacher who introduced me to the excitement of formal learning. Of all the memories of that school, many of them vivid and detailed, I cannot remember learning to read. I do recall that she employed the phonic system of instruction. She flashed the cards on which the letters of the alphabet were printed, and in unison we sounded them. In this respect, I went to school with a liberal "head start" from Mother.

My prejudice in behalf of the phonic system has been strong, but the method has all but disappeared. Here and there it is given a revival—frequently as a kind of curiosity. Our generation of Montana youngsters learned to "sound out" the words, and I cannot recall a youngster in the later grades or in high school who had any difficulty with reading. Spelling, furthermore, seemed to be an effortless and automatic by-product of learning to read.

The Huntley School student body included about a dozen pupils, ranging from the first to the eighth grades, all in one room. In some mysterious way, Mrs. Sommers sorted us out so that each youngster received his share of attention. The one-room school is not the brawling cockpit one might imagine. A small area at the front of the room was reserved for the group or individual whose turn it might be for recitation. Mrs. Sommers pitched her conglomerate classroom in low key, so it was not difficult to concentrate in spite of the hum of the education processes up front. Homework was not spared. I can recall eavesdropping on the recitations of the more advanced pupils, with the result that in later years there was much that came in the nature of review. I had somewhat surreptitiously borrowed instruction from that of Rudy Waal, Steve Osier and Carrie Franklin.

A brand of pipe tobacco marketed at that time was packaged in a gay candy-striped tin container, like a miniature picnic basket. It was the universal lunch box for schoolchildren. Neither Dad nor Grandpa smoked that particular brand, however, so my sister and I usually carried our lunches in gallon Karo syrup pails. In cold weather we ate in the schoolroom; when it was warm we sat outside, with our backs against the building.

The noon hour usually began with a brief period of determined bargaining between Roy Waal and me. Day after day, Roy's, Elena's and Rudy Waal's lunch boxes were stocked with the delicious *flatbrot*, which, frequently, I had watched their mother prepare. It consisted of a thin batter poured directly onto the top of the stove, cooked until small brown spots began to appear, then removed, cut into manageable sections and served with butter. In appearance, texture and taste it was not dissimilar to the thin bread found in Syria and Lebanon, but the Middle East product does not rival the Scandinavian, particularly as it was prepared by Mrs. Waal. In any event, I bartered portions of my lunch each day for generous slices of Roy's Scandinavian bread.

Steve Osier and Danny Pinkerman must have been five or six years older than I, so I was spared any need to struggle to maintain a neutral position in the bitter rivalry which existed between them. A number of school days were marked by vicious fights between Steve and Danny. They never fought on the school grounds or close enough to the building to invite intercession by the teacher. Rather, they had a habit of slipping unobtrusively into a deep ravine about two hundred yards east, and there the bloody struggles would occur. They must have loathed each other with an intense juvenile passion. They would not quarrel or fight with Rudy Waal or Bizgard Kappel, who were the same ages; nor did they bully us younger boys.

A fight between Steve and Danny did not begin with a slanging match or exchanges of insults. At some signal comprehended only by themselves, they would simply disappear into the gully and beat each other unmercifully. On several occasions the fights continued all afternoon. They would fail to return to classes after the lunch period, and the rest of us knew what was going on. A four o'clock, when school was dismissed, we would rush down to the ravine, to find Steve and Danny utterly exhausted, clothing ripped, bloody, but still attacking each other with undiminished fury. Once, these two arch enemies quietly retired from Sunday School to meet in "the gully of honor."

Roy Waal was the only boy of the immediate community who was in my age bracket and in the same grade at school, and we were good companions. Roy profited in all the lore of rifles, hunting, trapping and fast horses absorbed from his older brother, Rudy. I managed to hold my own, however, with second-hand tales of the railroad, borrowed from Dad, and embroidered for the occasion, and the vivid stories I had heard Grandpa tell—stories of his Missouri boyhood, of his experiences as a teamster and a streetcar motorman in Kansas City, or his brief years as a prison guard at the Colorado State Prison at Canyon Ferry.

Roy and I watched meadowlarks and curlews build

their ground nests and hatch their young. We killed rattlesnakes and fashioned bracelets by stringing the rattles together. We watched the absorbing processes of animal copulation, birth and death. We caught great bullfrogs out of the Whitewater, explored the hillsides for Indian tools and artifacts, and carved our initials in the carapaces of turtles. We found moss agates and speculated on their beauty should we one day afford the cost of having them cut and polished. We performed great feats of aerial daring and experiment by launching ourselves from the end of the hoist rope in the barn loft: taking off from the highest beam, swooping in a great arc at the end of the rope, then letting go at the precise moment to soar free and land in the big mound of hay at the other end of the loft. We experimented unsatisfactorily with parachutes from the peak of the barn to the straw pile.

Roy and I were devoted and pathological rock throwers. Small boys harbor a primordial attachment to a round, smooth stone, and we were no exception to the rule. The banks of the Whitewater had been denuded down to tremendous gravel beds—billions of rocks worn round and crudely polished by the gigantic churnings of the "Great Glacier" and by the erosion of wind and water. There Roy and I engaged in target practice for hours.

Rock throwing, and my expertise at it, got me into a slight squabble at school. I observed Ivy Osier going into the girls' toilet. Holding in my hand a small, round stone, I found the temptation too great. I was both startled and immensely pleased as the stone flew straight and true to vanish through the small star-shaped air vent in the side of the privy, then clattered and bounced about inside for delightful seconds, followed by agonizing shrieks from the startled Ivy. She emerged, asserting furiously that the stone had hit her. If it did, it was on a belated bounce when its impact would have been spent, but I was in trouble, nevertheless. When I argued unwisely that I had heard the stone bouncing about inside the toilet, it was obvious at once that I was the culprit. It cost me a couple of whacks with a ruler across the back of my throwing hand.

My first three or four years of school were thus spent at the modest little frame building a half mile from home. An intervening half century has not erased the sharp memories of Rudy, Roy and Elena; of Steve, Bertha and Ivy; of Helen and Danny; of Florence and Carrie Franklin; and of Margaret Busche. They were happy, rewarding years despite crop failures, drought, pestilence and numb despair. By any standards we were children of the poor, but we were not aware of it. Our lives and fortunes were full.

So the declining years of ranch life developed out of twin circumstances. That autumn after the barn had burned, Mother moved into Saco, ostensibly to guarantee Wadine and me a full and uninterrupted school term. At the Huntley School no classes were held during the severe months of midwinter. However, the disappointments and failures had overtaken the hopes and promises. Dad started working on the Great Northern for longer periods of time. We had begun the difficult process of tearing ourselves away from the land and beginning anew.

The struggle on the Montana land was one of inordinate and unbalanced odds. Agricultural science was not sufficiently advanced in the early years of the century to provide counsel for these new settlers by the Department of Agriculture, or the Extension Service and the state colleges, that the northern land would be more productive were it not put to the plow. That information came after the fact. It was splendid grazing land, and grazing land it should have remained, supporting cattle in a ratio according to the snow crop, the spring rains and the growth of the native grass. It is quite likely that as the thousands of acres were turned under by the plowshares, the soil was ready to produce not only the planned crops, but was equally capable of producing and reproducing the Russian thistle and serving as convenient breeding grounds for the locusts and other pests.

But the entire life on the land—human, insect, animal and vegetable—hung desperately on the whims of the weather. Two or three days of warm sun at precisely the right moment in early spring could produce an overwhelming crop of locusts or grasshoppers, hatching an extraordinarily high percentage of the billions of insect eggs implanted in the ground. An absence of rain in the period following the seeding of the fields meant a low degree of germination of the seeds and a stunted, irregular crop. If the fields did receive spring moisture and produced bumper crops, then the danger period came in late July and August, when the devastating hailstorms might crystallize out of the great towering thunder caps to pulverize field and pasture.

The risks were too great, the odds too long. It was not a case of tilling the fields with some degree of confidence that if that were performed with care and expertness the law of averages would provide a respectable return. The rule was quite the reverse: the chances of a rewarding harvest were a puny minority.

So these last American pioneers on the last frontier of the nation led harsh lives. They pitted knowledge and more of their sweat against the stubborn land. They stared unpredictable and extreme weather in the teeth. They reflected upon the whims of the deity, nature, or their own luck, which would lead a grasshopper swarm to *their* fields or direct a hailstorm to *their* land. They reflected upon and frequently cursed the economic injustice of the marketplace which usually lowered the prices for their harvests when the crops were good and had escaped storm and pestilence.

Insecurity was a stranger to me. There were love and laughter in the bleak and unadorned little house at the foot of the hill and facing innocently to the east, to compensate for the grudging nature of the land and its fits of harshness. But there was a deep and abiding sense of frustration, even for a child. I wanted to help, but I was too small, too young. Surely there was something I might do to help erase the fleeting evidences of despair which I saw on the faces of my elders. I recall the arms of my mother around me, holding me very close, when she discovered me one day laboriously struggling with buckets of water from the well—trying to resuscitate the withering plants in the vegetable garden. Mother frequently counseled that my most noble and appreciated contribution to the ranch would be the generous guardianship of my smaller sisters, but that seemed to be dull duty.

Perhaps this childish sense of frustration, stemming from an inability to serve parents and adults, is universal. Does the desire to be of service outdistance physical capability? It led me to all sorts of trial-and-error adventures: inexpertly castrating sheep and calves, experiments in irrigation and water conservation, milking cows with wrists not yet strong enough, riding untrained horses, bulldozing young steers, and trying out farm machinery and tools.

There was never anyone who could swing a hammer as Grandpa could. Under the tremendous blows a great steel spike would drive into board and timber. To this day, my hammer bounces futilely off the stubborn head of a ten-penny nail!

I dare say it was Grandpa who, as the family patriarch, established the unspoken and unwritten rule that adversity was not to be expatiated upon. It required no elaboration. The market and nature were not to be discussed in pejorative terms, and there was no need to curse one's luck. It was though nature had to be tamed and stared down. Let her devise all her capricious tricks, let her threaten to compound disaster; she would relent eventually when she discovered an undisturbed equanimity and unbreakable will. Gathering up the pieces, husbanding what remained or what little had been harvested, and planning for the next effort was our nepenthe.

In these circumstances the social graces of the frontiersmen were not overly developed. Our mother would frequently admonish us children at the table for a breach of manners with the remark that we were behaving like some of the neighbors. The language was often vigorous. Jim Pinkerman could manage to insert a cuss word into a request that someone pass the salt and pepper. He was the community's purveyor of dirty jokes.

Dad's use of profanity was strictly reserved for the Model T, a horse that refused to be harnessed for a day's work, a calf being taught how to drink out of a bucket, or for a cow which could (and would) wrap a long manure-laden tail around his neck during the milking. Otherwise, Dad's speech pattern was modest and comparatively pious.

Grandpa was, on the other hand, an expert "cusser" . . . not a swearer. Mark Twain would have said of him that he had both the words and the melody. His hyperboles and metaphors had grace and style. I never heard him invoke the deity or the Saviour, nor did I ever hear him make reference to parts or functions of the human body. "Son-of-a-bitch" was his best cussword, and it was usually preceded by a string of descriptive and highly accurate adjectival words and phrases. Thus a wayward horse might become "you sway-backed, broom-tailed, no-sense son-of-a-bitch." Grandpa rarely applied the expletive to a human. However, I do recall Grandma serving notice one day, in no uncertain terms, that she did not want to hear any more such talk, when he called the Methodist preacher from town "that trombone-playing, pious, hypocrite son-of-a-bitch."

Grandpa finally refused to go to the schoolhouse on those infrequent Sundays when the minister had alerted the neighborhood by mail that he would be there at the appointed hour of two o'clock in the afternoon. That permitted him to conduct his morning service in town, save the souls of the West Bench in the afternoon and get back to town in time for his Sunday evening sermon. He did, indeed, play the trombone—excruciatingly. He would pick up the long shining instrument, and without accompaniment, blow and bellow through a chorus of "Throw Out the Life Line" or "Jesus Wants Me for a Sunbeam." One day I noticed Grandpa grimacing in pain as the preacher staggered through his trombone solo. Grandpa's hands crept up stealthily and covered his ears.

The preacher was too much even for my tender

naïveté. He was awkwardly slick. There was forever too much talcum powder on his freshly shaved face. His suits were just short of the checkered pattern worn by traveling salesmen in the movies. He told unfunny jokes, and his appeals for "a generous offering" were based on the supreme need to aid Methodist missionaries in their efforts to rescue the Chinese from heathenism, mixed with a broad inference that a handsome offering in the passed hat would insure a good crop.

I have been startled with the realization that I was born at about that precise time in the early twentieth century to have seen this nation of ours engaged in four foreign wars, to have remembered all of them, and yet to have been either too young or too old to participate in any of them as a combatant. We Americans born in that brief span of years around the turn of the century and shortly thereafter are unique in having experienced more wars than any other generation of our country, which is perhaps only a sad commentary on this violent century.

Montana, in World War I, sent more of its sons into the armed forces, per capita, than any other state of the union . . . by far.

Before the Congress passed the Selective Service Act in May 1917, 11,709 Montana men volunteered for the Army and 1,862 voluntarily entered the Navy or Marine Corps. By the time of the Armistice in 1918, 39,271 young men had voluntarily enlisted in the Army, and several thousand more had sought out the recruiting offices of the Navy and Marine Corps. The proportion of enlistments to population exceeded by more than twenty-five percent the record of any other state.

But through a gross error, Montana's contribution to the military draft, in addition to those who had enlisted, was about twice what it should have been. The last census had been taken in 1910. The population growth in Montana between 1880 and 1910 had been a startling three hundred percent. The administrators of the Selective Service System erroneously took it for granted that this population growth had continued and they concluded that the population of the state was 952,474. Actually it was only 496,131—about half the estimate. Thus the figures of military obligation for Montana men were far out of proper proportion, but the quotas were filled. Out of every 10,000 citizens Montana furnished 796 fighting men. South Carolina, by comparison, recorded 296 per 10,000 population.

The volunteer rationing systems were scrupulously observed in the towns and on the farms and ranches. We cheerfully abided by the recommended sugarless, meatless and assorted other ". . . less" days of the week and month. Mother, Grandma and Aunt Cela knitted socks and sweaters and sent them to the collection points. We subscribed to the Liberty Loans and purchased the Thrift Stamps.

Young men of the community, from town and the ranches, began to appear in Saco, clad in uniform, on their last brief furloughs before journeying to the battlefields of France. The World War I uniforms were hideous and highly impractical "getups" obviously designed by some well-meaning executive in the old War Department for an army that was never intended to fight. They featured such incongruities as the wrap leggings, a tight high-collared tunic, and campaign hat. One of the first acts of the American soldier upon reaching the front was to remove and throw away the leggings. They tended to work loose with the slightest exertion, to leave the soldier trailing from his legs several yards of woolen khaki material.

But I took immense vicarious pride in the soldiers I saw in town. On several occasions long troop trains stopped to take a siding for another west-bound train or to permit the locomotive to take on water. I would join the pack of small boys who would dash to the station platform to wave admiringly at the sea of faces peering from the train windows. If time permitted we would run back across Main Street, convince the clerk in the Co-op that we wanted Bull Durham for the soldiers, spend our meager reserves, and scurry back to offer our modest gifts.

At the ranch I struggled with the big words and the foreign names in the Kansas City *Star* and Saco *Independent*, and I followed the big German offensive of 1917 and the Allied "big push" of 1918. Montana men were frequently mentioned in the action at Cantigny. Montana's old 2nd Regiment had seen action on the

Mexican border against Pancho Villa. The 56 officers and 913 men were no sooner at home and out of uniform than President Wilson summoned them back into service. A number of men of the 2nd were in the 3rd Machine Gun Battalion on July 15, 1918, when the German advance was halted at Château-Thierry. The 91st Division also contained many Montanans as it fought through the Argonne Forest.

The magazines of the war years frequently contained pages of patriotic stamps which could be cut out and pasted on correspondence. I was a faithful correspondent to an uncle in service, as I scrawled out my messages and decorated the envelopes with stamps bearing such exhortations as "On to Berlin", "Hang Kaiser Bill," "Smash the Hun" and so on.

The war stories of Belgian children impaled on German bayonets had a most profound effect upon me, generating a massive degree of loathing and hatred. In later years we school youngsters were told, or we read, that the Germans had not been guilty of such atrocities and that we had been taken in by "clever British propaganda." Then I was angry all over again. It seems that it required a good bit of my adult life to discover the truth about the World War I occupation of Belgium and to realize that the German ruthlessness, impersonal and institutionalized, did not include the premeditated murder of children. It occurs to me that Barbara Tuchman has set the record straight in her magnificent book *The Guns of August*.

By 1918, I was beginning to read laboriously from a

newspaper and I thrilled to the stories of Allied successes. I trotted along beside the Rainbow Division and flew against Richthofen. Grandpa had promised to take me into town for the Armistice celebration, but the day before, I came down with influenza, which was then sweeping the nation in a disastrous epidemic.

The Town

When we moved "into town" that first autumn, I had no idea that we were leaving the ranch . . . that a transitional process had begun. We returned to the land for several summers after that, and I spent summers with Grandpa after Dad had returned to railroading and we had moved to the Southern part of the state; but the ranch was no longer HOME with all the syndrome of permanency, stability and durability.

By this time, Uncle Johnny and Aunt Emma had withdrawn from the family pact, had sold their share of the land and the enterprise to Grandpa, and had returned to Missouri. Grandpa moved the headquarters of the ranch to Uncle Johnny's house and outbuildings on the southernmost portion of the 960 acres. Through the long winters to follow, our house, on the northern 320, stood empty, gazing silently across the basin toward the road. No sound came from the barn, the corrals, the granary, the chicken house where once there had been such activity.

Grandpa was to stay on in his grim contest with the vagaries of weather and market until 1924. When he held his auction sale and ventured to Texas, the few remaining neighbors followed the unwritten law of the grass prairie: board by board, sometimes room by room, gate by gate and beam by beam, they moved our buildings and added them to their own. Today, there is not a clue to where either group of buildings and structures once stood . . . not a trace of the cellar, the house, the privy, the well. The great rock on the hillside behind the barn, on which the lambs used to play, is still there, however; and I had no difficulty finding the old foundation to the barn which had burned that August night so long ago. Kicking and poking at the grass, I found an old tug chain, probably one on which Rex or Savage had pulled with such fury, and a little mound of earth yielded a rusted metal bar bearing the embossed words "John Deere." The fields and the once well-worn path to the well lay in mute desuetude.

Awe and some terror marked my first day at school in town. I would assume that the combined elementary and high school of Saco boasted an enrollment of perhaps 150 to 200 youngsters, but it had never occurred to me that boys and girls might be collected in such vast numbers. That school was a multitude of strange and slightly hostile faces, and neither the University of California nor Michigan State has ever rivaled the Saco school's numbers on that first day.

My first morning in the town school was traumatically engraved in my memory by a fire drill. The building was suddenly seized by the frightening and earsplitting din of the fire gong. The children in my classroom, well trained in the procedure, quickly put aside their books, papers and pencils; arose and filed out the door, with the teacher taking a position of command in the hallway. I simply could not grasp what was going on, and consequently I ventured hesitantly in the wake of all the others. In the hallway, the principal, Mr. Wampler, was standing beside my teacher, and as I stumbled by he pointed at me and said, "That boy is going to burn up!"

Terrified, I rushed home at noon to ask my mother, tearfully, what that man could have meant when he said I was going to burn.

My initiation into city school was complete, painful, sometimes bloody, but rewarding. Within two weeks I had been unmercifully beaten by virtually every boy in the class and by some from other classes, but with the stern urgings and reprimands of Grandpa I had sought out return engagements and had given a rather respectable accounting of myself. Within a few days I was a full-fledged and accepted member of the urchin pack.

That first winter in Saco was a sort of perpetual fiesta for a nine-year-old ranch boy. I learned to ice-skate on a pond of water which invariably collected and froze between the railroad embankment and the street on the south side of the tracks. We skated on Beaver Creek, which flowed past the town about a half mile to the southwest. There was sledding every afternoon after school down the steep railroad embankment and out into the town's main street. One had to time his slide to avoid the automobiles and horse-pulled vehicles. I recall Clyde (his last name forgotten) skidding into a team of dray horses, his sled splintered to bits, and coming out of it with nothing worse than a broken arm.

Part of the ecology of Saco, abetted by the inventiveness of small boys, produced a singular sport, which, hopefully, neither time nor contemporary sophistication has eliminated. It bore no particular name, but it involved a variety of competition and activity having to do with mud. The town was built on a low and semiswamp flat, which held tenaciously to its moisture because of poor natural drainage. The area was commonly known as "the Saco flats" or "the gumbo flats."

For the uninitiated, gumbo mud is the most devilish and impossible mixture of clay and water on the face of the earth. Saco's unpaved streets were rendered into bottomless wallows, slick as a pit of soap and sticky as molasses.

But gumbo in the hands of small boys is quite another matter. Its consistency, by adding either water or a little dry material, could be controlled and made into a substance slightly less solid than modeling clay. A round ball of gumbo mud could be thrown with all the speed and accuracy of a baseball, and it had the altogether delightful property of flattening out like a fritter and sticking to its target with an incomparable stubbornness. In our gumbo battles both sides were often incapacitated by laughter as one of the combatants peeled a pancake of mud off his face. In the absence of an engagement between two opposing armies, the exercise sometimes turned into a melee of each boy for himself, or target practice in which we plastered and decorated sides of buildings with hundreds of precise, round gumbo pancakes, which hung there for a few days and then dropped off, leaving no stain or blemish.

With amazingly modest loss in life and limb we played another game native to most Montana towns, where the railroads maintained stockyards for the loading and unloading of cattle. Saco's stockyards comprised several acres of pens, gates, chutes and alleys. The outside and inner pen fences or walls were topped by catwalks about ten or twelve inches wide. The installation was an ideal facility for a hair-raising brand of tag featuring hot pursuit along the catwalks and breathless leaps to gates which might swing the pursued safely to another catwalk and leave the pursuer hopelessly foiled. I have often concluded that Hitchcock's imagination does have limitations, after all; else he would certainly have filmed a chase sequence in a stockyard.

I remember rather vividly the night of Prohibition, which, according to the history books and *The World Almanac*, occurred at midnight January 15, 1920. Grandpa came in from the ranch for the occasion, to pay his respects to the establishment which had enjoyed his patronage and whose atmosphere had pleased him. As I recall, he made no effort to "lay in a supply" as so many did in the final hours prior to the nation's great illusory experiment with abstinence, virtue and social uprightness. Rather, Grandpa hooted at the new law and predicted that it would never work. He went out that evening and returned rather early. Dad, as I remember, was working the four-to-midnight shift at the depot. I listened eagerly while Grandpa supplied Mother with the details of the celebration which was going on downtown.

Prohibition, I judge, was never given a complete trial in that section of Montana. Several of the old saloons went out of business and closed their doors forever, the establishments converted to other retail enterprise and the proprietors turning to other pursuits. At least two of the town's saloons, however, became "pool halls": the Western equivalent of the speakeasy—although there was no particular necessity to exercise restraint. The town drunks never sobered up, and whiskey remained an item easy to come by. The pool halls no longer served it by the drink but rather by the half-pint, pint or quart. Much of the product was moonshine, but Canadian whiskey was usually in plentiful supply. It came across the border thirty miles to the north and made its way into the towns along the "high line" via the network of country roads.

From some backyard shed or basement, my closest friend, Kenneth Ball, and I obtained several muskrat traps that winter, and we sought to make our fortunes along the banks of Beaver Creek. Each afternoon we would hike through the snow to the stream and inspect our traps. I believe we caught two before concluding ultimately that fur trapping was a vastly overrated enterprise. In thousands of newspaper and magazine advertisements, furriers invited the small boys of the nation to reap fabulous rewards by sending in muskrat, beaver, rabbit, weasel and skunk hides. We skinned our two muskrats, stretched and hung the pelts and sent them off to one of the advertisers. Weeks later, we received a check for $1.05!

Kenneth Ball was a remarkable boy. Over the years I have wondered whether he grew up with a full development of the noble character he possessed as a small boy. Kenneth's father was in a Canadian prison, convicted of killing another man in a quarrel over the ownership of some cattle. The story was that the shooting occurred almost precisely on the Canadian border and that George Ball had been apprehended trying to carry the body over to the American side of the line, where cattle quarrels were more frequent and where the punishment was far less stern than in Canada. In the years that I knew him and his younger twin brothers, Clyde and Clarence, the father was never mentioned, and I must have had the good grace never to inquire. Mrs. Ball managed to support her family by taking in washing. I can remember the lights always burning in the Ball home, as she washed and ironed late into the nights.

One summer I was permitted to spend the Fourth of July in town and stay with Kenneth. I think the big attraction was a baseball game which both of us wanted to see desperately. Dad had given me a small sum of money for some fireworks, and Kenneth had about an equal amount. We pooled our resources and purchased one magnificent rocket which had the weight and appearance of a most spectacular instrument and which would crown our private fireworks show. At dusk, therefore, after hours of anticipation and following all the elaborate preparations and cautioning the younger twins, Clyde and Clarence, to stand back, we undertook the firing of our rocket. With great care we stood it on its launching stick and inclined it at the proper angle. Kenneth applied the lighted match. The fuse caught and began to spew fire. Then with a great whoosh the rocket took to the air, streaming a long tail of sparks and red smoke. But something had gone awry! For some inexplicable reason its guidance system faltered and lowered the spectacular trajectory. It dipped sickeningly back toward the ground, recovered, and streaked like a great comet unerringly down the middle of the street. Far down at the end of the thoroughfare was the town's electric supply system, consisting of one large gasoline-driven generator. Straight and true, our rocket headed for the generator house. Aghast, we watched it streak precisely through the big front door of the plant, into the incredible areola, and dissolve inside the building in a shower of sparks. Then the operator of the electric plant dashed out of the building, stopped and waited for the explosion, and looked up and down the street. Several other people joined him and they all began gesticulating, pointing this way and that. To our relief the knot of people dissolved and the engineer went cautiously back to his generator. Kenneth, the twins and I crept from behind the shrubbery to the other side of the house.

Kenneth was the most poised and calmly detached boy I ever knew. I am sure he had suffered deeply because of the imprisonment of his father and the agony it had brought to his strikingly beautiful mother. Kenneth's mother and my parents permitted neither of us to loiter along Main Street after school, and in order to bask in his companionship it was often necessary that I help him empty tubs, clean up the washroom or deliver and pick up the laundry, after I had ticked off the modest list of chores at our house. Whereas I might have had some inclination to participate in the customary mischief of small after-school urchins, Kenneth was uniquely above the foolishness, idleness or the gutter talk and curiosity of boys. He was much too wise for all that, and both of us, with ranch experience, were quite sophisticated about the mysteries of sex and childbirth.

Kenneth's room was a treasure mine of books and magazines on fishing, hunting, woodsmanship, exploration and outdoor adventure. Both of us learned to make a fire with a bow and spindle of wood. We wished repeatedly that our town had a Boy Scout troop, but we had a copy of the manual, and it was our conviction that we might have had a dozen or so merit badges immediately. We particularly loved to read about and discuss the science and art of trout fishing, although neither of us had ever seen a trout. The waters near Saco contained only lethargic carp.

I recall vividly Kenneth's stern counsel which he delivered me regarding a schoolmate, Dale Brown. Dale was a fiery redheaded and freckle-faced youngster, considerably shorter than I, but he was coordinated like a young tiger. For whatever reason, I must have been anathema to him, because his favorite sport was beating the daylights out of me. I had no particular dislike for him, and although I frequently came close to mastering him, in the end he would come off the undisputed winner. It was a frustrating situation.

Quite solemnly, Kenneth impressed upon me one evening that I simply had to make the supreme effort and "whip" Dale Brown once and for all. He was convinced that I had only to vanquish him in one climactic engagement to insure permanent peace.

I agreed, albeit with some misgivings.

Kenneth arranged the promotion and attended to details. Consequently, after school the following day I found myself in a circle of spectators, facing my antagonist on the snowy field. This encounter was, indeed, unique. My previous bouts with Dale had occurred with no advance planning and certainly without publicity. They were impromptu affairs. This one had been guaranteed to be decisive.

Perhaps it was that day in that empty lot that I made a discovery about myself: I was stronger and immune to physical pain if I was concerned or angry. In the dozen or so fights I had had with Dale I could never get sufficiently aroused. I was invariably embarrassed, chagrined, humiliated, but I had always had the feeling that it did not make much sense—that it was really rather silly.

This day, however, I had somehow worked up a fine charge of adrenalin, and I was determined to do injury to that freckled face across the ring.

It was by every count the best performance of my nondistinguished career as a pugilist. The fight went on for some time. I tasted the saltiness of blood in my mouth and I saw it streaming down Dale's chin from his nostrils. I fought as Grandpa had urged me to fight: no grappling, no wrestling, no rolling about; avoid your foe and hit with all your strength and fury. Finally, I sensed that Dale was defeated, but would he—could he—acknowledge it, as the local custom demanded? I thought of how much more punishment I might have to give him to force him to accept the humiliation. At last, he crumpled in the snow, covered his face with his hands and nodded his head.

I stood there for a moment, mildly aware of the cheers and congratulations—utterly consumed by a bitter inundation of remorse and sympathy. I wanted desperately to put my arm around him, help him up and tell him that I was sorry, but the rules did not permit that.

I was not a fighter. I did not have the instinct. It was a losing proposition either way . . . humiliation on the one hand or remorse on the other.

Dale and I, however, became friends, and I think he knew how I felt.

Years later, on the first day of classes at college, I sat

in the lecture amphitheater for freshman zoology as Professor Sterling checked the roll of his new charges. He called out, "Dale Brown!" I turned to see from whom came the responding "Here!" and it was the same fiery-haired, freckle-faced friend of the Saco years.

We saw Dad only occasionally that winter. He had decided to tide us through by working as a relief telegrapher on the Great Northern. With no seniority, of course, he was dispatched to whatever town on the division where his services were needed. As he transferred from one short-lived assignment to another, he would usually stop off at Saco for a day or two.

It was about this time that Dad began to be a much more interesting person in my developing judgment. He rarely came home without a new book, and his selection was invariably spendid: Jack London and Mark Twain, particularly. He sat at the big round table with my sisters and me and drew animals, buildings, railroad engines, and sketches of mother in response to our enthusiastic requests. He was a fine natural artist, but to this day he has steadfastly refused to try his hand at painting.

Dad always smelled like a railroad depot. The railroads of that era universally stocked their stations and offices with an inexpensive ink. It came to the depots along the line from the main warehouse in St. Paul in powdered form, contained in small packages. The agent or operator would frequently make up a batch of it by pouring the powder into a container and adding the required amount of water. That ink had a singular odor, and it caused every station, every freight office, every ticket office in America to smell the same. It was not unpleasant . . . but mildly pungent. I always liked the odor of Dad's clothing.

I had discovered that Dad was a jokester and a punster. Ours was a good-humored house, as Dad teased our mother and she graciously accepted the role of the foil. I remember Dad's quip one night on the ranch when he said he had figured out a new brand for the livestock: "Two lazy-two P."

It was perhaps that same winter, 1920, when Dad brought home one day a curious package of coils and knobs and said I might go with him that evening as he delivered them to the house of a neighbor. After dinner we walked a short distance through the streets, the snow crackling underfoot, and arrived at the friend's house. I sat and watched as Dad and his friend connected the wires and the strange instruments, adjusted earphones on their heads, and gently moved a little handle. They smiled with satisfaction and nodded to each other. Although Dad worked in Morse code he could follow the gist of a conversation or transmission in International Code. Finally, he clamped the phones over my ears, and I heard, for the first time, the strange beeps coming mysteriously out of the night. Dad said the transmission was from a ship somewhere off the West Coast . . . far out in the Pacific.

Dad became a genuine radio enthusiast. Several years later, after we had moved to southern Montana, we owned the first radio receiver in town. That set boasted a loudspeaker, and on the cold, clear winter nights KDKA, Pittsburgh, would come piping in, and we got to know the Night Hawks from Kansas City and Bill Hay from Hastings, Nebraska. Our living room was usually filled with neighbors and townspeople who dropped by to hear radio for the first time.

I suspect it was the next winter in Saco that Wadine and I were introduced to the movies. One night per week, films were shown in a little hall just off Main Street. With what wondrous anticipation and unbounded enthusiasm we followed the serial *Winning of the West* with Art Acord . . . in weekly installments, ten cents!

Perhaps the level of our sophistication was revealed by an incident involving me, the handle of a broken fly swatter, and electricity. A bulb had burned out and Mother was in the process of installing a fresh one, but I came by at that point and inserted the end of the fly-swatter handle in the socket. There was a flash of blue flame, a snap of electricity, and all the lights in the house went out. Mother was convinced—and with some anger, I might add—that I had blown up half the power supply of the town and that demanding officials of the company would be at the door any moment, exacting their punishment and penalties. So for several weeks we were back with kerosene lamps.

Ultimately, the meter-reader of the power company knocked at the door and inquired of my frightened and humiliated mother why she was not using electric light. Protecting me, she said that they simply would not work. He deftly slipped a new fuse into the box, and we were transported back into the electrical age. I was back in my mother's better graces.

I discovered the town library, and began inter-
spersing the classics with novels and the pulp periodi-
cals. To please Grandma, who came into town from the
ranch occasionally to spend a day with us, I read the
Bible, a book at a time, making notes on the chapters
and passages which I most enjoyed. I never hear one of
the Psalms but what I am transported back to those
raw winters and mud-congested springtimes of Saco.

It was March 1921, and we three children were
moved across town to stay with another family because
Mother was summoned out to the ranch. Grandma was
ill. Mother was waiting for Wadine and me at the
schoolhouse one afternoon, and she had been crying.
Grandma had died of pneumonia! I think it was Andrew Strommen who had brought Mother into town in
his car and was waiting to take us back to the ranch.

Grandpa was throwing hay to the livestock when we
arrived, and I joined him. He put his great hand on my
head and brushed my hair back but said nothing. The
soft darkness of early spring was settling down on the
hills and around the ranch buildings.

I followed Grandpa to the house and then to the
shed, where he took the lantern from its nail on the
wall, lit it and returned to the barn.

"We have to lay your Grandma out," he said, as he

removed the screws from the hinges of the barn door and handed the lantern to me. He carried the big door to the house and rested it on a pair of saw horses in the parlor. Clean and freshly ironed sheets were draped over the improvised bier awaiting the arrival of the casket from town.

All the neighbors came for Grandma's funeral. She lay there, smaller and more frail than in life, her long black eyelashes resting peacefully on her cheeks.

The service concluded, we filed out and prepared to follow the hearse to the cemetery on the hill overlooking the Saco flats. Only Grandpa remained behind. Through the window I saw his tall frame standing unmoving over the coffin. Then he bent down to kiss her face. He closed the casket and walked from the room.

The procession of cars swung out of the farmyard and down the lane. I sat beside Grandpa. Once he broke the silence, when he put his arm around my shoulder and said, "Your Grandma was pretty today, wasn't she, my boy?"

The sun was shining brightly as we stood there on the crest of the hill in the bare and forlorn little cemetery and saw Grandma lowered gently into the earth. But the wind, gusting and whipping down out of the northwest, denied the sun its warmth. It picked up the words of the graveside service, the short prayer, the recommendation of Frances Walden Tatham to God, and the benediction, and carried them on down the Milk River valley and across the flats.

We did not see Grandma grow old. It was charac-

teristic of her that she would give her life to the frontier. But her spirit was not sufficient unto the cruel
persistence of the March wind. March was the month
most feared. The sun crept back from its southern
sojourn, vaguely promising April, but it vied with the
wind. It was winter's last weapon—sharp and angry.
It cut down young and old, animal and human; and
plant life was held in its grip . . . withered . . . inert.

Doc Minnick always said that March was the killer
month. He had observed how the ranchers were
tempted, come March, to throw off the impossible and
confining layers of clothing with which they had con-
tended through the long winter. Clothing in those
years was invariably heavy and bulky, coarse and unmanageable. One went about like a padded Man-
churian peasant. It was impossible to raise the arms
above shoulder level because of the great wad of clothing that tended to accumulate at the base of the neck.
The leg could not be lifted high enough to get a foot
into the stirrup because another bundle of under- and
outerwear gathered at the crotch. Grandpa said that
half the winter was spent putting mittens on and off in
a constant compromise between warmth and dexterity
of the hands. Urination was a function to postpone
until the last excruciating moment, because it meant
buttoning and unbottoning the series of trouser vents.

Feet, hands, noses and ears were the inviting targets
of frostbite. Most of us wore a woolen helmet which
slipped down over the face, leaving a slit for the eyes,
but which protected the nose and ears. Woolen mittens
inside leather ones protected the fingers, provided we

were not forced to remove them to manipulate nuts and bolts and more subtle farm machinery. We borrowed from our Norwegian neighbors a custom which protected the feet. In late fall, the manes and tails of the horses were combed and trimmed to yield a generous ball of horsehair. The hair was then stuffed into a felt slipper, and the foot, with a wool sock on it, was gently introduced into the nest of horsehair. Within a few hours, the horsehair matted firmly and conformed to the shape of the foot, giving a sure protection against the coldest weather. Over the felt slipper we wore overshoes.

One of the many advances in American agriculture has been bestowed, therefore, by the textile industry, which, in recent years, has developed the splendid lightweight winter wear. It has increased the mobility of the American farmer manyfold.

Dr. Minnick was the noble, generous, unfailing public servant to Saco and its hinterland. My three sisters and a whole generation of that far-flung and dispersed section of Montana were brought into the world and nursed through its harsh vicissitudes by him. I see him vividly . . . the tall, lean, bent frame of the man striding along a Saco street, lugging the ubiquitous black bag. Or I see him through the windows of the ranch house, huddled in the seat of his buckboard, urging the horse on through the snow, as he journeyed up or down the lane, responding to calls.

Doc was a reserved man. He had little time for long consultations. His bedside manner was one of perfunctory efficiency and firm low-key orders. Invariably, his first words to the patient were, "How's your bowels?"

In the case of emergency, it was necessary for the rancher to race into town on horseback to summon Doc Minnick. Somehow, the ranchers on the east and west benches, up the Whitewater, on the Saco flats and along the Milk kept mental note of his going and coming. As the rancher raced toward town he would stop at an occasional farm house to ask if the Doc had been by. Frequently, he would be found not too far away.

My horse, Ted, had been wind-broken on a furious emergency ride into town in search of Doc Minnick. Ted was never capable of galloping very far after that.

Saco was no exception to the small-town phenomenon of harboring one self-appointed feminine chairman of everything. Meredith Willson did not do her injustice or overdraw her in *The Music Man*. Mrs. Snyder— we shall call her that—was small and plump, forever overdressed, supercharged with energy, and the repository of most of the virtue and civic-mindedness in town. She was also an overtime gossip.

It was Saturday afternoon, and a troop of us small boys were rollicking down the board sidewalk of Main Street, teeming with its usual Saturday commerce. Ahead of us, on the principal street corner in town, in front of the Co-op Store, Mrs. Snyder was talking energetically to two other town ladies. As we approached from one direction, a mongrel bitch dog appeared from the side street with a male in determined pursuit. Literally at the feet of the three ladies, the two dogs were joined in their unseemly act. Bravely Mrs. Snyder and her companions ignored the commotion going on about their skirts. The incongruity of it was devastating! To us urchins it was inconceivable that Mrs. Snyder could ever have been witness to the copulation of dogs . . . which under the best of circumstances is one of nature's less inspiring arrangements.

Then the street was transfixed as the male discovered himself unable to disengage. The two animals set up an infernal outburst of howling, barking, yapping and shrieking—skittering about and among the ladies. One of the women began beating the dogs with her purse, and that only compounded the commotion. Ranchers, cowboys, tradesmen and we boys stood in incredulity as the distasteful, but hilarious, little drama was played out, with someone mercifully dragging the two dogs around the corner and out of sight. Mrs. Snyder flipped the fox fur over her shoulder and hastened up the street.

The next time Grandpa was in town I gave him a detailed account of the incident, and he bent over with laughter.

May Day, in those innocent years before the proletariat turned it into a brash and chauvinistic holiday, was touchingly observed by the youngsters . . . at least, in our town. It had more currency in Saco than in any

other community I have ever known. Somewhat surreptitiously, we boys put aside the more predictable
pursuits to labor absorbingly over our May Day baskets. With glue, scissors and watercolors we fashioned
a basket for the "girl of our choosin'." It was filled with
candies and small gifts and carried stealthily, with
pounding heart and nagging trepidation, to the front
door of the girl's house. Never, by our local rules, did
the generous gift-giver reveal his identity. That was
part of the game. Carefully, the handle of the May Day
basket was fixed over the doorknob, then you knocked
loudly and ran hell-bent for some predetermined
hiding place.

I was singularly faithful to my fair Helen. Each May
Day, I brought my heart and my basket to Helen
Peterson's door and anticipated the next day at school,
when I would watch her intently studying every boy in
the class for some clue to the identity of her admirer.
Desperately, I wanted her to guess that it was I, but
simultaneously I was almost panic-stricken by the
thought. Alas, I fear I was much too impassive. I am
sure Helen never knew. One spring, she thanked Lee
Taylor for her May Day basket!

During one of those Saco winters, I experienced my
first nongifted, nondedicated teacher. I remember neither her name nor what she looked like. I know only
that there is an entire school year missing in my memory and that for the first time school was not an exciting, rewarding, stimulating adventure. Through the
years of elementary and secondary school, in seven
different communities, I was fortunate in knowing only

one other mediocre educator, and I was in her charge for no more than a few months.

The classes, of course, were always small or modest, and the deportment of the pupils was exemplary by today's standards. It had to be. We youngsters were well policed. There was literally nowhere we might go to lose our identity. Every individual in the entire community, rural and urban, knew our names or he could find out quickly, which meant that our parents had endless sources of information concerning our whereabouts and our behavior.

For good deportment there were very definite rewards, in school and in the community at large. The smart-aleck disturber of the peace never came off well. He was put in his place in a way and with an emphasis excruciatingly embarrassing for everyone there.

One day in class I was indulging in a bit of "brattishness"; annoying other youngsters and acting the clown. Miss Ellis, my teacher at the time, and one of my best teachers, finally walked down the aisle, stopped at my desk and stood regarding me for a long moment. Then she said, "Chester, if you ever do or say anything that is really clever or funny, we will all laugh and enjoy it; but so long as you insist on acting like a boob, all we can do is pity you." I heard a few snickers from around the classroom. She let the words sink in and calmly returned to her desk.

There was no P.T.A. or similar organization, official or otherwise, to whom a complaint might have been taken that Miss Ellis had called me a "boob," had embarrassed me before the class and had done irreparable damage to my precious id. My parents would not have protested had there been one, for they subscribed to the law of averages in which ninety-nine times out of a hundred the teacher was justified.

There were sterner punishments in reserve in the principal's office: hours after school, loss of playground privileges, written reports to parents, and even a razor strap or stout cane. The adults of the town and ranch community had an effective and noncomplicated system of punishment and reward. You were told that you were a "good kid" and "nice to have around"; or that you were "a goddamned little piss-ant of a brat and get the hell out of here!" The well-mannered youngster was taken into adult conversation and was bestowed with adult trust. We were rarely without spending money in our pockets, by virtue of the errands we ran for adults who genuinely liked us: unhitching and caring for a rancher's team of horses as he drove into town, delivering groceries to the townspeople or running telegrams from the depot to addressees, washing windows, cleaning basements. My pride knew no limitation when the blacksmith hired me occasionally to turn the bellows and otherwise assist him. Frequently, the proprietor of the livery stable employed me to water horses and pitch a bit of hay to them.

It stands to reason that there have been improvements in education processes and techniques in the past forty-five years or so. Our visual aids, I fear, were limited to the blackboard and a few maps or the globe. Today's school plants are certainly better-equipped. Textbooks are more stimulating, and a greater abundance of knowledge is readily available to the pupil. There are perhaps more first-rate teachers than ever before.

I am not certain, however, that there are more dedicated teachers today. They did not evacuate the building en masse on the stroke of 3:15 in the afternoon or queue up at the check-out window twenty minutes before quitting time. They were the first ones at the school in the morning and they were the last to leave. They were not the products of the "education factories" of our state colleges and universities, with their quotas of courses in education psychology, playground administration and classroom discipline. They were not inconsequential or impersonal little units of a "system," but they were genuine parts of the community, and they were "the school" insofar as the people of the community were concerned. The principal usually constituted the entire administrative establishment, and his contacts with the teachers were personal and direct. He did not resort to memos, directives, guidelines and countless emissaries.

The teacher's imagination was free to take flight, to prove itself by trial and error. She was a free agent. She did not have to pick her course among the school board, local politicians with axes to grind, the P.T.A., the N.E.A., departments of state education, and scores of community groups—all insisting on their little packages of dogma and orthodoxy. Now a teachers' labor union has been added to the list, and it too has its suffocating code of "thou shalt nots."

My teachers, very likely, were not that gifted, but

they were that dedicated. They cared and we knew it. That, I suspect, was the difference. They cared and we responded, usually with the best that was in us.

The two mediocrities who supervised two brief stages of my elementary education were, I am convinced, of the identical stripe of those found in our large urban school systems today and who were the subjects of a particularly devastating study and report recently. It was found that the communications line of education had been cut in the city classroom, not because the pupils were incapable of learning, but rather because the teacher *thought* they were. Those two dreary teachers in my experience were too greatly motivated by the prior conviction that we children of that simple, uncultured and primitive environment could not possibly be sparked by the desire, the excitement and the capacity to learn.

In January 1920, Aunt Cela, Mother's younger sister, came in from the ranch to spend a few days with us in town. Aunt Cela had taken nurses' training a few years earlier at a hospital in Minot, North Dakota; and after her marriage had terminated in divorce she lived with Grandma and Grandpa—managing Grandpa's household for many years.

A morning or so after Aunt Cela arrived, she hurried Wadine and me off to school, explaining that Mother was not feeling too well. Sister Marian was removed to the house of a neighbor.

At noon, Dad was waiting for Wadine and me at the front door of the school, and we were told that we had a new baby sister. Peggy had arrived!

It was incredible how these sisters appeared without undue commotion and no prior announcement. Both Peggy and Marian were surprises. Several years earlier, Wadine and I had been elated one morning with the announcement that we had permission to walk over to the Waals' that morning and play there with Roy and Elena—all day. I recall that this sudden permissiveness on Mother's part was a bit strange, since she was forever reluctant to let her children complicate the routine and the household of a neighbor, but Wadine and I dashed off to the Waals'. Late that afternoon when we returned, Dad met us in the barnyard, and we were allowed into the house to see Marian, all pink and fast asleep in her improvised crib fashioned out of a properly padded and decorated clothesbasket.

Dad and Mother's brood was expanding, and he had elected definitely to terminate his career as a rancher and return to railroading. As long as he was going to resume railroad telegraphy, he reasoned, life would be more comfortable and rewarding on the Northern Pacific, which traversed the southern part of the state, as opposed to the Great Northern, which ran through the northern tier of counties. I daresay Dad thought of the fishing streams of the mountainous southern counties.

Dad left to begin his long climb toward seniority

on the Montana Division of the Northern Pacific, and we did not see him in the months that followed, but letters and postcards and gifts arrived frequently.

In the spring, Mother told us children that we were going to leave Saco to rejoin Dad and that our new home would be Willow Creek. Eagerly I found a map of the state and pointed out to Kenneth where we would make our new home. Kenneth saw immediately that Willow Creek was located on the Jefferson River at the foot of the Tobacco Root Mountains and at the very western end of the long and beautiful Gallatin Valley, about seven miles from the point where the Gallatin, Madison and Jefferson rivers join to form the Missouri. Kenneth and I talked of the trout fishing I would experience, the mountains I might climb and the camping trips I would know. He promised that he would come to visit as soon as he could.

Our departure was set for the day following the close of the school term. Mother had packed our belongings in boxes and trunks, and most of them had gone on by freight. Dad had written that he had found a house in Willow Creek and that all was in readiness. He would be working there for a few weeks, until the vacancy in the Willow Creek depot was bid in by the operator with the most seniority.

Grandpa and Aunt Cela had come into town from the ranch, and the goodbyes had been said. We would return for a visit the following summer. Sadly, I waved farewell to Grandpa as he climbed into the farm wagon and departed.

The train, on which we would ride with passes, was

due in Saco at about 10:00 P.M. I borrowed a small handcart to deliver our suitcases and bundles to the depot that afternoon. Finally, my sisters were aroused from their naps, Mother dressed Marian and Peg, Wadine and I divided the remaining valises, and our journey began. I set the bundles on the porch, turned out the last light and closed the door. Clustered around Mother like a band of small gypsies, we set off through the darkened streets.

A new life—new surroundings, new influences, new interests—had begun. As exciting as the future promised to be, the final closing of the front door to that little house on the unassuming little street was not without its grave symbolism. I was quite aware that I was leaving a town and a country-side that was home —that the past had been pleasant and so very familiar; the future was uncertain.

At the depot our baggage was properly checked through to Willow Creek. The second-trick operator on duty wished us farewell and sent his best to Dad. A train whistled its disconsolate approach.

The door of the little waiting room opened and there stood Kenneth and his mother. Mrs. Ball had put aside her work, and Kenneth had fought off sleep that they might see us off.

The great clanking and puffing locomotive loomed out of the night, and the mail and baggage cars slid by, hissing steam from their couplings. Then the first coaches rolled past, the interior lights revealing faces peering out at us and human forms draped in all manner of uncomfortable sleep. The officious conductor, blue-suited, watch-chained across ample abdomen, silver-buttoned, and regulation-capped, stepped down, and the brakeman set the rugged iron step on the platform.

Kenneth thrust out his hand and said, "Be sure to write me about the first trout you catch. I hope it's a big one!" He slipped a small package into my hand . . . a Boy Scout knife!

Mother carried Peggy and all the various comforts and necessities that went with her at that age. I was in charge of Marian's pudgy little hand, with firm instructions to get her safely aboard just ahead of Mother. Wadine, with a small suitcase in one hand and the birdcage containing Tweetie in the other, was to follow Mother, and I would bring up the rear.

I had rebelled to the limit of Mother's patience against taking Tweetie, but the canary was Wadine's prized possession, and Tweetie was not going to be left behind! I think I was partially mollified by the ultimate decision that I would not be forced to carry Tweetie and his cage—that Wadine would have to struggle with the cumbersome burden. Apparently, at eleven, I had reached that age at which conformity takes on premium value and I was convinced that carrying a birdcage, with a chirping and nervous canary inside it, was several notches below my dignity. Without complaint Wadine accepted responsibility for Tweetie's safe transport, and she discharged it without particular incident. From inside his hooded cage, the canary chirped occasionally throughout the long journey.

We stowed our suitcases and bundles and settled down for the first leg of the protracted adventure . . . our exodus.

This was the golden age of the railroads, but north-south service in Montana certainly did not qualify. East-west service was excellent, with all three of the transcontinental lines operating first-rate trains: the Great Northern with its Empire Builder, the Milwaukee with its Hiawatha, and the Northern Pacific's North Coast Limited. The three companies operated a number of other trains as well.

But the schedule for the trip from Saco to Willow Creek, a crow-flight distance of some two hundred miles, was incredible. We would journey westward to Havre, arriving there at some painful hour of the early morning, wait interminable hours for the train which ran southward from Havre to Helena, getting into Helena at about noon the next day, where Dad would meet us. There we would board the Northern Pacific southeastward to Logan, and thence westward about fifteen miles to Willow Creek. But we children had been told that Dad had planned a great holiday for us—we would stay over one night in Helena to see the sights! Our total net traveling time would be almost forty-eight hours.

We waved our goodbyes to Kenneth and his mother as the conductor called out his practiced "booooo-rd" and the engineer responded to the high sign. With a slight lurch the train began to move.

The yellow and brown-trimmed depot slid silently past, revealing the boardwalks, the storefronts and the lights of Main Street. There was the Co-op on the corner, the railroad embankment down which I had sledded on happy and boisterous winter afternoons, the bank, the pool hall, the barbershop, the tumbled ruins of the old mercantile which had burned to the ground one December night.

The engineer splintered the night with several long blasts, indicating that he now meant business, and we picked up speed. The last lights of town receded, and we glided across the Saco flats and thundered over the old iron bridge on Beaver Creek, beneath which I had skated and trapped for muskrats. Miles to the north, had he been watching, Grandpa might have seen the train as it sped on toward Malta and Harlem, Dodson and Havre; for I had seen train lights many times from the ranch.

It was the end of a way of life, an experience, an era. Although we visited Grandpa and Aunt Cela briefly for two ensuing summers, we would not come "home" again. The familiar and the predictable vanished into the darkness of the June night. A shower of sparks leaped from the funnel of the engine, and they cascaded back like fireflies, glancing from the windows of the coaches, etching brief journeys in the blackness, and glowing for a moment in the reeds and rushes of the right of way. The engineer wailed his mournful farewell song, and it echoed for an instant in the folds and gullies of the benchland then fell asleep.

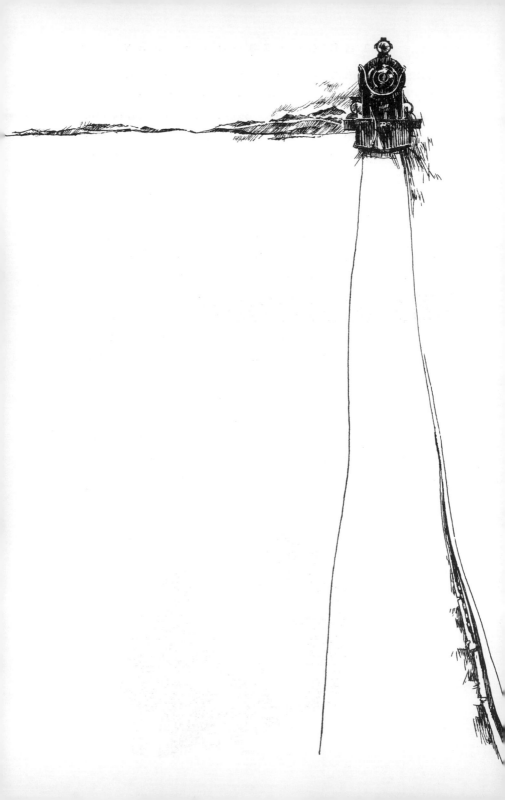

The Railroad

We awakened to the sounds of commerce, the shouts of baggage men, train inspectors, and the contented puffing of switch engines. We were at the station in Great Falls!

The long hours of waiting in Havre had finally ended and we had fallen into exhausted sleep as the train carried us southward around the Big Bend of the Missouri.

The activity at the Great Falls station was astounding: cars and trucks and pedestrians seemed to be going in all directions. It was obvious to me that Great Falls, about which I had heard Grandpa talk so frequently, was a tremendous metropolis!

From persistent questioning of Mother, I was excitedly aware that somewhere shortly south of Great Falls we would see the mountains. The train would actually go through a mountain range between Great Falls and Helena. This was to be the day that the mountains would assume form and shape and character, in contrast to the faint blue line of the Little Rockies on the far western horizon. Would the mountains really be as they were invariably pictured in the books and magazines I had read? Would the great evergreen forests be as serene, would the streams froth and tumble and leap down the gorges, would the lakes be that cool and idyllic, and would the great granite peaks thrust up toward the sky . . . or was it all some photographic trick?

The mountains had become something of a modest obsession. They are yet! Seashores, plains, deserts, sun-washed and sea-skirted islands, riverscapes— none compares with a mountain . . . a Montana mountain. Its alluvial fans sweep down toward the valley, which it invariably dominates. A mountain or mountain range is forever so magnificently and perfectly based, all in proportion, its shoulders and snow crown in dimensional harmony with the massive and gently ascending foothills on which it is set. From a distance, the timber belt is a band of color: a great blue-green sash, and soaring out of it the craggy slabs and domes, the spires and monoliths . . . naked . . . stark.

Traveling toward a mountain and ascending its gigantic base is a transition from the general to the particular. The forest belt is a splash of color. But the scrub pines and spruce become thicker and taller, water gushes from the side canyons, the mountain meadows appear, ringed with nervous little quaking aspen, and finally the forest begins. Its carpet is deep and silent. Fallen timber sustains the delicate ferns. And it is cool beyond belief . . . cool, and utterly at peace with itself, resigned to its cycles of growth and decay . . . life and death.

At last the train moved out of the station, swung

around the falls of the river and raced across the plateau. To the east I caught glimpses of a mountain range, and to the southwest there was another, their peaks snow-splotched and shining in the morning sun. Then we descended into a gorge, twisting past outcroppings of rock, the flanges of the wheels screaming against the rails. A stream appeared on the right, and through the fresh spring foliage I could see it dancing over its stony bed, collecting itself in dappled pools, resting a moment, then furiously boiling over its obstacle and resuming its chase.

Halfway through the canyon the train made its stop at Wolf Creek. On either side the mountain walls rose upward and disappeared in a wilderness of fir and spruce. The rush of the stream could be heard up and down the gorge. The aspen, mountain ash, chokecherries and willows sported their new June growth, and the air was carbonated with vitality.

Wolf Creek shall forever be special in my memory. It was my personal "Gates to the Mountains."

Dad was there to meet us in Helena.

Baggage, children, adults crowded into a taxi (another first), and we arrived grandly at the Eddy Hotel. What a sorcerer my father was to arrange everything and to know his way around in all this confusion and excitement. The elevator whisked us to our floor, and from the window I peered down into the main street of Helena . . . Last Chance Gulch.

A streetcar, jangling its bell at the tangle of vehicles, whined and complained up the crowded thoroughfare. Above the din I heard the shrill voices of the newsboys hawking their copies of the *Independent* and the Butte *Miner*. Multitudes of people were intent on their errands, coming and going. A young boy on a bicycle swerved assuredly through the traffic, and I was envious of his confidence. How could he be so detached from all the confusion going on about him? Did he really know where he lived? Could he find his street, his house, in all this commotion . . . in all this endless and bewildering expanse of city . . . without stopping someone for directions? How could people swing on and off the streetcar with such air of easy assurance?

Helena, Montana! Capital city! Metropolis! Baffling, wonderful and frightening!

We ate lunch in the dining room of the hotel, a thousand times more grand than the Saco grill to which Grandpa had taken me, and its menu indecipherable. How could anyone know that he was to receive a hamburger steak if he ordered the Salisbury Plate?

Later that afternoon we boarded the streetcar for a journey about the city. We rode past the state capitol, with the mountains rising up behind it. We passed Wesleyan College and the sky-reaching minaret of the Shrine Temple.

It had been a grand and incomparable day. There had been too many new sights and sounds, but I would sort them out in good time. Tomorrow we would continue this splendid journey. It was not over yet.

It was late afternoon when we arrived at Willow Creek, and it was what I had almost dared hope. Smaller than Saco, it nestled snugly in the narrow western extremity of the broad Gallatin Valley. The Jefferson River cut through a mountain barrier from the west to join the Madison, and the Gallatin. Towering above the western valley rim was the Tobacco Root Range and its principal peak, Old Hollowtop. Southward, the hills with the wheat fields gleaming on their slopes, rose in endless series, to lose themselves ultimately in the jumbled mass of the Madison Range. To the north, across the river, frowned a rampart of cruelly gouged and eroded foothills, and the basin sprawled to the east.

The area surrounding the little town was greener and more lush than anything I had ever seen. Water seemed to come from everywhere, gushing down from the hills and mountains to join the river. Small irrigation ditches ran through the town, and watering a garden or lawn involved only a simple process of damming the flow and permitting it to spill over.

Trees and shrubs grew in profusion. Five minutes after we had arrived at our newly rented house in Willow Creek, I was ecstatically exploring the highest branches of a great cottonwood which towered over a corner of our yard.

The creeks were lined with trees, and along the river there was a veritable jungle. Volunteer trees and shrubs grew at the edges of the farm fields and on the banks of the irrigation ditches.

Saco and its vicinity, like the ranch, were barren by comparison. The rainfall was far less and there was no irrigation. The shrubbery in the front yards frequently was killed off by the deeply penetrating frosts, and I am sure that the community was still too new, too young, too experimental to permit the growth of trees. They would come in later years, when a second generation had accepted the one-time frontier settlement as its home. Town and city trees indicate a sense of permanence.

Mountain distances are misleading to the newcomer. I asked a new young friend how far away were the rugged hills to the north. I think I had confidently said that I was going to explore and climb them, but that was deferred when he said they were on the other side of the river and about twelve miles distant. Mountains always appear to be much closer, to the unpracticed eye, than they actually are.

Many times I was to hear the story of the ubiquitous Pat and Mike who apocryphally had come to Montana and learned that a certain mountain range was twenty-five miles away. A few days later, Pat observed Mike on the bank of an irrigation ditch, removing his clothes. When asked what he was doing, Mike replied that if those mountains were twenty-five miles distant, he was taking no chances trying to jump the irrigation ditch.

That was an exciting boyhood summer. The surrounding hills were explored and the cliffs scaled. My new companions and I roamed through the woods along the river and gathered watercress from the tributary creeks.

In the irrigation reservoir just beyond a ranch on the edge of town, I learned to swim. That opportunity had been denied me in Saco because we had always moved back to the ranch in the spring, the moment the school term ended, and the water in Beaver Creek was still much too cold.

On the way to the swimming hole we spent hours scaling a great sandstone cliff in which the swallows nested. The formation was so soft that the swallows could burrow into the face of the cliff to make their nests. Laboriously we carved steps into the face and dug out perilous trails over which we ran and leapt.

Dad's tenure at the Willow Creek depot was brief, and he was dispatched to the town of Roberts, Montana, sixty miles or so south of Billings. Mother packed our clothing one day, and we boarded No. 220 to visit Dad.

The journey was uneventful, but Roberts was a more exciting town than Willow Creek. It lay at the very base of the Absaroka Range, and Rock Creek came boiling down through the heart of the community . . . crystal-clear and icy cold. A few hours after our arrival Dad took me fishing, the first of many such expeditions we would share over the years to come. On the bank of the creek, Dad taught me how to tie the leader to the line and the hook to the leader, how to hold the elbow close to the body and cast out into the stream. The trick was to make the fly look as harmlessly natural as possible, as though it had just landed on the water or were floating innocently down the stream. It was no good pulling a fly against the current because no self-respecting trout would ever be misled by it. Dad explained that one of the most rewarding techniques was to look for eddies or pools along the bank, in which the water swirled back under overhanging trees, and to cast a fly into the shadow. However, he cautioned, trout were unpredictable. There would be times when they would leave the pools and sport themselves out in the swift water of the main current. When they were in swift water, the thing to do was wade out carefully on a bar or riffle and cast into deeper water just downstream.

Dad struck out to fish upstream and suggested I might try working downstream.

Clumsily I tried casting the fly where I wanted it to go. I would need much practice.

Then an explosion occurred at the end of my line! The sharp tug was unmistakable, and he came out of the water, dancing on his tail. Now it was all real. What had the stories in the books and magazines said . . . ? "Don't haul on them, let them have their head but keep the line taught, gently and patiently work them toward you, spin the line with the left hand through the right and control the line between thumb and forefinger . . ." Several times I worked the rainbow up to my feet and he took the line back into deeper and swifter water. How firmly did I dare resist his pull before the leader would break or the hook tear from his mouth?

Finally, the fish was spent and he came in almost docilely. I lifted him onto the grass.

Dear Kenneth.

I caught my first trout yesterday . . . three of them. They were rainbows. Wish you were here.

Later that summer, Dad worked for a few weeks at a little mountain town called Pony, situated at the very base of Old Hollowtop in the Tobacco Roots. Alone . . . importantly, excitingly, memorably alone . . . I rode No. 219 from Willow Creek, changed to the little spur train at Sappington and arrived at Pony to stay with Dad for a few days. Again we fished the streams, and one night we were invited to go by car to Potosi Springs. The Model T labored and struggled up the narrow canyon, with Old Hollowtop gleaming in the moonlight. We stopped at a point where water gushed out of a tremendous rock formation at the side of the road.

We walked a short distance and came to a crude log vat in the ground. Someone . . . no one knew who . . . had fashioned a sizable rectangular tank out of logs and lowered it into one of the pools of water. Two wooden troughs hung over one end of the log tub. From one trough, ice-cold water tumbled into the receptacle; from the other poured a torrent of hot water. The bather could control the temperature of the pool by merely swinging the troughs about, forcing either the hot water or the cold to by-pass.

We splashed about and soaked ourselves in the hot

mineral water, then dressed, and rode back down the canyon in the brilliant moonlight.

The early 1920s marked the demise of the hot-spring era of Montana. When the construction of the Northern Pacific was finally concluded in 1883, one of the first promotion programs of the new transcontinental line was that of attracting tourists to the water spas of Montana. The Northern Pacific, child of the German-immigrant financial genius Henry Villard, envisioned a series of fashionable watering places, in the best traditions of Baden-Baden and Carlsbad. The railroad built and operated several of these resorts and encouraged others. For several decades the cities of the Eastern seaboard heard of the delights and comforts and health advantages of Broadwater Springs near Helena, Bozeman Hot Springs, Chico, Corwin, Pipestone, Hunter and a number of others. Great hotels were constructed and the plunges were built under glass domes. Mud and mineral baths of several varieties were widely advertised.

Potosi Springs was too remote for this sort of attention and development. It has remained for the simple convenience of the people in the area.

But the twenties saw the decline of the hot-spring resorts. In the prohibition era, some of them enjoyed uncertain patronage when an occasional adventurer would buy or lease the establishments and turn them into bootleg palaces. Sooner or later, however, they would be raided and the doors would be locked again. Gradually the fine hotels, with their great dining rooms and spacious verandas, were left to fall apart. Some of them burned to the ground. The roofs fell in on the pools and plunges, and the one-time social centers were forgotten.

In Willow Creek, I came to know "tourists." It was a word rarely used in Saco. Travelers from other parts of the nation or the world who came to visit Glacier National Park usually traveled by train, or if they toured by automobile, they did not venture eastward into the prairie country. But southern Montana boasted a better through highway, such as it was. It was bravely marked as "The Yellowstone Trail" or "The Lewis & Clark Route," and it attracted the early tourist adventurers in their Pierce-Arrows, Overlands, Reos, Hudsons and Maxwells. Willow Creek was on the main highway. It ran through the single commercial street of the town, with its feed store, drugstore, and post office on one side, and grocery, blacksmith shop and bank on the other. In summer the cars, piled high and laden with camping equipment of all description, bearing strange license plates from faraway places, and carrying bone-weary and patience-robbed people who wondered how they had become ensnared in such an adventure and how they could most expeditiously get out of it, rolled through the little towns of the Gallatin Valley. After a hard summer rainstorm, the farmers along the route invariably hitched up a team of horses and profited well from hauling the unsuspecting tourists out of the mud. At evening, tourist campers could usually be found at the roadside where the highway crossed a creek or river.

The Montana farmers and ranchers were generous

with tourists, however—very few of them posting their land and warning fishermen or trespassers off the property. That hospitality still exists. In spite of the damage inflicted on fences and gates left open, the campers and the fishermen and hunters are welcome, and free to explore as they choose.

Although I invested no time in reflecting upon it, it was obvious to me that there was a difference in mood and temperament between the communities of southern Montana and the one we had left to the north. The frontier had vanished quickly after the advent of the Northern Pacific. People in the southern towns and communities were friendly and generous, but they were not the friends and neighbors of the northland, whose fortunes and experiences were, in the main, one's own. The pace of the new life seemed somewhat more brisk; slightly better roads permitted a bit more mobility; the newspapers published in Butte were, at least, more detailed and sophisticated than the Saco *Independent* but not any more reliable; and there was more contact with the outside. The State College at Bozeman, fifty miles or so to the east, was spreading its influence.

The Gallatin Valley was one of the old counties of the state and had been settled early. In 1865, Nelson Story had brought the first herd of Texas cattle up the long Texas trail and into the valley. Story and other early settlers were quick to realize the agricultural potential of the area.

Bozeman, the county seat of Gallatin County and

situated at the eastern extremity of the valley, was originally called Farmington. On February 9, 1869, its name was changed to Bozeman City in honor of John M. Bozeman, who had given his life in active service during the Indian wars not many years earlier.

We were destined to live in Willow Creek only a few months. In midwinter, Dad bid for the third-trick post at Logan and won it. It appeared likely that he might have sufficient seniority to hold that position for a while because who would want the midnight-to-eight shift in the dreary little railroad town?

We were a railroad family . . . railroad children. In the early years of Dad's return to the Northern Pacific we grew somewhat accustomed to moving about, following the uncertainties of the seniority system. Any telegrapher with considerable seniority set in motion a whole chain of relocations if he was "bumped" out of his post by someone with more seniority or if a job on the division was closed out. It was a ruthless and sometimes harsh system, but those were the rules and no one complained very bitterly. As the years passed, Dad's seniority increased and the result was that we began to reside in places for somewhat longer periods of time. Thus we moved about, from Logan to Big Timber, from Big Timber to Norris, from Norris to Whitehall, from Whitehall to Bozeman. After I left home, Dad and Mother and my sisters lived in Williston, North Dakota; Sidney, Montana, and Reedpoint.

My youth, from eleven to twenty, was spent along

the right of way of the Northern Pacific. I came to know the towns, the rivers, the mountains, the valleys. I learned the incredible distances.

Butte, the copper capital of the world then, did not engulf me with awe as Helena had. I had lost my innocence. Butte was the unquestioned metropolis of Montana, population 65,000. All through the twenties it was a roaring camp, secure of its reputation as "the richest hill on earth." Out of the shafts and tunnels beneath the city poured a constant stream of copper ore, embedded with sufficient quantities of silver, lead, zinc and other minerals to pay the overhead. In three shifts per day, the Irish, the Cousin Jacks, the Bohunks, the Polacks, the Dagos and other assorted ethnic groups of miners went down the narrow shafts, to the 3,600-foot levels and beyond, then dispersed through the labyrinth of horizontal tunnels, or drifts.

The mines bore the esoteric names of the Alice, the Emma, the Mountain Con, the Elm Orlu, the Blackrock, the Hibernia, the Netty, the Cora, the Belle, the Orphan Girl, the Minnie Jane, the Ophir—belying the high accident and fatality rates, the hard work, the dust, and the stifling heat which seeped into the drifts from the bowels of the mountain.

To pull the ore cars from the faces of the drifts to the vertical shaft, donkeys were used frequently. These little animals were snow-white, for they had never experienced sunlight. They were born, they worked and they died in the deep recesses of "the hill."

The city sprawled haphazardly along the side of the mountain and spilled down onto the flats; an ugly jungle of derricks and typical jerry-built mining-camp structures. Nowhere was there a tree or a bush to relieve the harsh monotony or mask the cruel pastiche of dirty brick, rusted steel and weathered board; nor was there a lawn anywhere. The "big stack" of the smelting plant at nearby Anaconda had, for years, discharged its lethal loads of arsenic and other noxious poisons into the atmosphere, killing off the vegetation in the entire Butte-Anaconda basin.

The social and diversionary establishments of the city also operated round the clock. Crap tables, roulette wheels, the blackjack and poker games, in scores of establishments, never ceased. At every window in block after block on Mercury Street, the girls tapped gently at the male passers-by. On Arizona Street and Montana Avenue the raucous sounds of miners at play continued into the small hours of the morning, seven days per week. Butte paid no attention whatsoever to the nation's capricious experiment with Prohibition. Innocent shoe stores frequently opened into generous back-room saloons, speak-easies with their characteristic little slots in the doors faced boldly upon the streets, and the restaurants served ice and set-ups as the patron was seated. Mudro's Grill, in which it was widely asserted that Jack Dempsey had a financial interest, was a fine dining establishment . . . each table isolated behind its none-too-discreet red velvet curtain. (Dempsey actually did not have a financial interest in Mudro's, but he was a great friend and a faithful customer.) Walker's Grill advertised throughout the state that for all cooking and frying, it spurned everything but butter. The Rocky Mountain Café in Meaderville, the Italian quarter, was world-famous and did not close its doors until the late fifties.

With a firm and benevolent policy of "local interests only," the city was ruled by Chief of Police Jerry Murphy. On the most bitter days, with the temperature at 30 or 40 below, Jerry would direct traffic at the busy and treacherous corner of Montana and Park, his great mustache drooping with icicles. He was the law. He enforced, interpreted and made much of it in the street. Litigation and argument in the county and state courtrooms up on the hill were confined to the endless disputes over mineral rights. Criminal law was Jerry's exclusive province.

The story was that one day in the twenties, a fleet of long black limousines drove into Butte and parked ostentatiously at the curb. Jerry sauntered over and asked the identity of the "man in charge." The leader of the group said he was from Chicago, that he guessed he was talking to Chief Jerry Murphy and that Jerry would be interested in a proposition he was carrying from certain well-known people back in the Midwest metropolis. Jerry calmly replied that he would not be interested, that the visitors were welcome to look around a bit but they would have until five o'clock that afternoon to get out of town . . . and stay out.

Throughout the Prohibition era repeated attempts were made by the mob elements of the East to gain control of "the action" in Butte and turn the city into a protected gangster headquarters, but all efforts failed. A hometown entrepreneur could operate any sort of establishment he might elect, but no outsiders were permitted.

Butte, in the twenties, was confident that its civil-war era was ended, that its destiny was manifest and that the rich veins of copper in the hill were inexhaustible. The city was only a few years out of its uncertain past, in which it had endured one of the great internecine struggles of American money and politics and in which the people of the community had been forced to line up for one side or the other. Butte had been the center of politics and copper, and as rough and unprincipled as it was, it is to the everlasting credit of all those involved that, with rare exceptions, the issues were ultimately resolved politically. There was very little gunplay.

Much of the southern half of the state, in the early twenties, was arousing itself from the wars of the copper kings, centered in Butte, but which had spread out to the state administration, the judiciary, the legislature, to small mining operations, to logging camps, cattle ranches and county governments. The conflict had been waged daily in the rival newspapers: the Butte *Miner* and the Anaconda *Standard*. The struggle was the recent history of a region. As late as the last third of the twentieth century, those who aspired to political office and leadership in southern Montana would be forced to take a position in respect to "the Company."

Growing up in that climate and in that area meant an absorption and an assimilation of our recent past. Fragments of the whole story were still told in passionate and unrestrained language. Some spoke in awe of the terrible power which had been wielded in Butte, others took delight in recounting how ambitious and selfish men had destroyed themselves. There were tales of tremendous courage, of little men standing up to the giants, only to be crushed and ruined.

In January 1926, Dad bid in the second trick at Whitehall, located forty miles east of Butte, and his seniority was sufficient that he held the post for four years. Consequently, my secondary education was derived in one high school, with the exception of the first four months. I went to Whitehall High School longest of any school or institution in all the years from first grade through university graduation.

Whitehall was a Butte satellite. We youngsters joined Butte student organizations and engaged in mutual enterprises. Whitehall families frequently shopped in Butte; we drove into the city occasionally to see a football game or a show. Mother was in a Butte hospital for an extended period one winter, and on weekends I would take Wadine, or Marian, or Peg to visit. During the summers, Whitehall youngsters frequently worked in the copper mines, but Dad and Mother would never have tolerated that, so I always found employment on a ranch.

The sin and vice of Butte were not hidden from youth. We were free to come and go in the gambling halls, the speak-easies, dance halls, and presumably in the bordellos. In the saloons we were permitted to order beer, but no hard liquor. We were tolerated briefly at the gambling tables, before the dealer good-naturedly suggested we make ourselves into spectators. Many times we walked along Mercury Street and exchanged mild vulgarities with the highly painted prostitutes in the window.

"How much?" we would ask.

The temptress would lift her skirt and hold up two fingers.

"We don't want to buy it . . . just rent it!" someone would shout.

Often the madam would stick her head from the door and tell us to get our skinny little asses off the street.

One evening a group of us boys had driven into Butte to see a movie, and as we left the theater we encountered Slim. I have no idea what his surname was. However, Slim had been a notorious bootlegger and pimp in Whitehall at one time and had moved on to richer proprietorship in Butte.

Slim recognized several of my companions and insisted that we must all come up to his "club" on Arizona Street, where he would buy us a beer. With some misgivings we trooped along, climbed the stairs and entered Slim's establishment. A bar ran along one end of the room, a number of tables stood about, an orchestra occupied the other end, and the center of the room was reserved as the dance floor. On the walls and from the ceiling hung forlorn and grimy papier-mâché decorations of one kind or another. Cartoons and prints appealing to assorted voyeurism were prominently displayed.

We stood at the bar as Slim poured out the beer.

Presently we were accosted by several girls who insisted that we must dance with them, and Slim, from behind the bar, ordered the girls to "get those boys out on the floor and show 'em a little fun."

The boy in whose father's car we had driven into Butte was Harry Burgoyne, a handsome and athletic lad, the favorite of the schoolgirls. Finally Harry, embarrassed by the entreaties of the dance-hall girls and thinking it was the easier way out, let himself be dragged onto the floor. For the first few steps things went well and the girl was a model of decorum, then she began to respond to the urgings and shouts of Slim. She wiggled her behind, then her torso, then both. She executed bumps and grinds. Grimly, Harry was determined to see it through and brave it out. The girl then clutched Harry closely, and with one hand lifted the back of her skirt and tucked it in her belt. Harry was unaware that his companion was dancing about the floor with her bare bottom exposed to the roaring and applauding crowd. Finally, she seized Harry's hand and placed it emphatically on her buttocks.

That was too much. His face crimson, Harry pushed her away and bolted toward the door, turning and waving to us to follow him if we wanted to get back to Whitehall.

None of us had appreciated the show. I recall that we saw nothing humorous about it. We were embarrassed. I had the uncomfortable conviction that I was in a situation well beyond my years and sophistication. To the guffaws of Slim and the hoots and shouts and whistles of the audience, we stumbled out of the "club" and departed for the innocent climate of our little hometown.

Thus the past and the untempered present of Butte were unavoidable. To endure the city, we had to understand it, and to understand it, we had to know its history. Butte was not an accident. It had developed in a natural way out of the passions and unbridled desires of men. It was what they had made it.

The story of the Montana copper wars, far from being a digression, rather is part of the personality of this region of America. In the twenties it was not only the northern grassland that was emerging from its frontier cocoon; changes were occurring in the more populous southern section as well.

From many sources, piece by piece, I soaked up the rich history of the city. It became part of me, as it was a part of the environment and culture of the region.

Forty years earlier, in 1876, Butte paid no attention to the arrival of an immigrant Irishman, Marcus Daly; charming, witty, garrulous, a talented businessman and a prospector with a shrewd sixth sense which told him where the deposits lay and in which direction the veins of mineral ran.

Previously, from 1864 to about 1885, Butte's modest

economic welfare had been tied to silver. Small silver mines dotted the mountainside, and the copper content of the ore was dismissed. Daly, by some arcane mental process, deduced that the mountain at the backdoor of the wretched little mining camp was loaded with copper. He put his money where his hunch was, and purchased the Anaconda silver mine for $30,000. Striking out laterally into the hill from the central core of the old silver mine, Daly tapped the richest deposit of copper the world has ever known.

By the late 1890s, Daly's fortune was tremendous. So was his ambition, and there were new financial zeniths to be realized. In 1898, Daly negotiated a financial pact with the Standard Oil Company to form one of the largest trusts in the history of this country, controlling 75 percent of the stock of the original Anaconda Company as well as that of other companies. It was called the Amalgamated Copper Company.

But the fortunes of Butte and Daly had attracted others, including another gay and reckless adventurer, a German-Irish-Jewish mining engineer, Frederick Augustus (Fritz) Heinze, who openly acknowledged that he was a financial pirate. Arriving in Montana in 1889, he made friends and money. His plan of piracy in Butte was initiated. Quietly, he purchased small plots of land, complete with mineral rights, around and about Daly's rich copper mines. Heinze's next move was to "tidy up" the legal front. He advanced generous loans to a number of judges and put some others on his payroll. That accomplished, he set off his bomb in Butte. Heinze went into the courts, seeking cease-and-desist orders against Daly and Amalgamated, on the grounds that the rich copper veins were "peaking" in his small plots of land and that Amalgamated had no right to pursue its lateral drifts under his surface property. Amalgamated was ordered to cease and desist, while Heinze feverishly began extracting the ore from his congeries of small holdings. Simultaneously, Heinze fulminated and preached, struck off pamphlets, and bought newspaper publishers to enlist the support of the people of Montana and Butte in his holy crusade against "foreign combines and monopolies." To make his point more effective and attractive, he raised the wages and shortened the hours of the miners, pointing to Daly as the unscrupulous profiteer and the usurer of the lives, the happiness, the health of honest working-men.

Amalgamated, however, fought back. It raised the wages and reduced the hours of its own men. In its main offices at 25 Broadway, New York City, batteries of lawyers were engaged in the preparation of counter-suits and strategies to get the cases out of the jurisdiction of the Butte and Montana judges.

The Butte story grew more absorbing.

War broke out underground. The miners of either the Daly or Heinze camp would frequently burst through a subterranean wall to find themselves cheek to jowl with workmen of the rival company. They fought each other with live steam, hot water, dynamite, chunks of ore, shovels and slaked lime.

The litigation accumulated. Heinze enlarged his legal staff until thirty-seven lawyers were working, at one time, on more than a hundred cases, aimed directly or indirectly at Daly and Amalgamated.

Late in 1903, Amalgamated launched its counter-offensive, backed by all its economic power and combined indignation. It closed down every one of its operations in Montana: the mines, smelters, lumber-mills, ore railroads, company stores, refineries. Overnight, twenty thousand men were out of work, and panic struck the city of Butte and spread throughout the state.

Amalgamated then announced its terms: Heinze to sell the units of his small-plot constellation which formed the basis for his lawsuits against Amalgamated; *and* convening of the state legislature in special session to adopt a new law permitting a party to a lawsuit to remove its case to another jurisdiction if it was convinced, or had any evidence, that a judge was prejudiced or was in the pay of the opposition.

The governor of the state at the time was Joseph K. Toole, a Democrat and anti-Daly, but he was trapped. The twenty thousand men in the state, out of work, were demanding that something be done; and merchants, tradesmen, bankers, businessmen in scores of Montana towns were applying pressure upon the governor, declaring that Amalgamated's demands were for nothing more than simple justice.

Toole reluctantly called the legislature into special session and with greater reluctance signed the hurried bill into law. A few months later, Heinze, his legal and extralegal strategies played out, sold his collection of little mines to Amalgamated for $10,000,000.

Daly made very certain that the people of the state understood that it was only his generosity which had provided for that amount, and that it was strictly "nuisance value" money.

Thus Amalgamated had established its reputation in the state. A Supreme Court decision in 1911, ordering the dissolution of trusts of the Amalgamated type, did nothing to minimize the power, real and purported, of the company. The Court decision was followed by a reorganization of paper and names, and the Anaconda Copper Mining Company made its entry into the political, economic and social life of Montana. Quickly, it became known as "the Company."

But the wars were not over yet. While Daly and Heinze had been struggling to the death, yet another fortune seeker had begun to prosper. From banking, real estate, lumber, mining and refining, an unobtrusive Scotch-Irish Presbyterian, William Andrews Clark, put together a fortune and quietly made his entrance into the affairs of Butte and Montana.

The story, as I heard it, alleged that Daly simply could not tolerate the reserved and abstemious "Scotsman," and they had traded insults one night at a gathering in Butte.

The day Montana became a state, in 1889, William A. (Bill) Clark made it known that his crowning ambition was to serve in the United States Senate as a lawmaker from Montana. Daly hooted at the suggestion and vowed that he would see "Bill" Clark in hell first. Perhaps he did.

This stage of the Butte wars became rougher, more

scandalous and more bitter than the long fight between Heinze and Daly. It was not to be ended until 1911, and it featured wholesale buying of votes and judges and politicians, theft of ballot boxes, the murder of an election judge, and unprecedented bribery. Again, the war spread throughout the state and beyond. It caught up unsuspecting people and forced them to decide in favor of one or the other.

Chris Connolly in his book, *The Devil Learns To Vote—The Story of Montana,* says that Daly spent about two and a half million dollars in his personal efforts to keep Clark out of the United States Senate. Former senator Burton K. Wheeler of Montana told me that the figure was a fair estimate.

In that period, of course, prior to adoption of the Seventeenth Amendment, United States senators were elected by the state legislatures. Clark embarked upon the project of getting himself elected by the Montana lawmakers. I was told the story by some of the legislators involved: how Clark's sons were overheard saying that they would send the "old man" either to the Senate or the poor farm, as they brashly bought votes. The payoff was arranged. The seduced legislators were told to be in their rooms of the hotel at a designated hour and to leave their transoms open. The talk and the gossip and the rumor of buying votes was one thing, relatively harmless; but the actual deed of exchanging money was something else, not to be witnessed. The appointed hour arrived, and over the transoms of the carefully noted hotel rooms were tossed fat bundles of twenty-dollar bills.

Meanwhile, Daly had discovered what was going on and hc clcctcd to fight fire with fire . . . cash with cash. Daly's men descended upon the capital and belatedly began to buy votes to guarantee Clark's defeat.

However, Daly either launched his counterattack too late or failed to raise the ante sufficiently, for in the legislative session of 1899, after eighteen days of balloting and acrimonious charges and countercharges, William A. Clark was elected to the United States Senate.

But Daly was not through. Quickly, he secured the signatures of twenty-seven members of the legislature to serve as affiants on a petition to the Senate, demanding that Clark be barred by the sergeant at arms and asking the Committee on Privileges and Elections to undertake an investigation. Clark was turned back at the door of the Senate, and the committee opened hearings.

For days the Clark and Daly forces appeared before the panel of senators, each indicting and denouncing the other. The record is all there in the files of the Senate: three thick volumes of it. The senators were familiar with cases of political chicanery and fraud which marked the nation's civics throughout that unrestrained period, but the Clark-Daly feud of Montana surpassed them all. There was rather substantial evidence that Clark had spent as much as three-quarters of a million dollars securing the votes necessary to guarantee his election. Finally, he acknowledged that it had cost him about $275,000.

It was too much for the committee. It found Clark

guilty and voted to void the title to his seat in the Senate.

Still Clark was not finished. Before the committee could file its report to the Senate, Clark issued his resignation to the press but withheld the filing of the required papers to the Montana authorities. The Montana legislators anticipated another Senate election at their next session in Helena.

Clark's men went to work on a plan. The governor of Montana was Robert B. Smith, avowedly anti-Clark and pro-Daly. An elaborate plot was devised, which consisted of enticing the governor to a dazzling social function outside the state. The unsuspecting governor accepted the invitation, and Clark's men shadowed him to make certain he arrived safely at his destination.

The moment the governor stepped across the Montana line, the word was flashed back to Helena by telegraph. A Clark aide hurried to the office of Lieutenant Governor A. E. Spriggs, who was as pro-Clark as the governor was anti-Clark. Clark's resignation from the United States Senate was handed to the lieutenant governor, who accepted it, honored it, filed it and promptly appointed Clark as the new senator from the State of Montana.

Governor Smith rushed back to Helena, and another long and involved saga of litigation was inaugurated. The governor and the lieutenant governor were now in the thick of it.

For eleven years the battle ebbed and flowed, flared up and died down; but the Montana seat in the Senate remained vacant. Finally, time and fate appeared to intervene to resolve the matter. Clark and Fritz Heinze joined forces, and as though this were too much to bear, old Marcus Daly wearied of the fight, fell ill and died. Spriggs and Smith had been replaced by new leadership, and the membership of the Committee on Privileges and Elections had altered. So it was that Clark took his appointment back to the Senate and was finally seated in 1911.

The lights blazed that night in the William A. Clark mansion on New York City's Fifth Avenue.

At some point in these years, the Montana State Historical Society, obviously aware that a lot of rich product was going into the obscurity of the grave along with those who had been involved, began to gather material. On limited resources, it has functioned well. Historical roadside signs and markers, now present throughout the state, are the work of the society, and they are the envy of the nation for their characteristic humor and wit.

But with virtually no funds, the Historical Society, at first, enlisted the aid of school authorities and schoolchildren. History and English classes were urged to enlist as contributing historians: sending to the society in Helena any essay, note, hint or suggestion of historical value.

So it was that we schoolchildren of south-central Montana ultimately assumed credit for touching off a fascinating row, ending in a rather unique ceremony.

High up in the southern extremity of the Tobacco Root Range, where it depreciates into a diastrophic massif of huge denuded hills, separating the Jefferson and Madison watersheds, lies the sad little town of Virginia City . . . population not quite two hundred by the last census. Virginia City was the second territorial capital of Montana and site of the famous Alder Gulch gold rush. At its brief zenith about 1868, an estimated fifty thousand prospectors and Chinese coolies tore at the sides of the gulch and washed most of it down the coulee through the sluice boxes.

In the course of events at Virginia City, a respected and widely admired local citizen by the name of Henry Plummer was elected sheriff. Not long thereafter the stagecoaches, carrying the fortunes of gold dust and nuggets down the Jefferson Valley to the main stage-coach line, began to experience an exceptional rate of holdup incidence. Sheriff Plummer and his possemen, time after time, rode back into Virginia City, their horses lathered and lame, reporting how they had chased the bandits down Ruby Creek, along the Jefferson, only to lose them in the woods and thickets.

The fortunes of the stagecoach line sank so low, and the intelligence of the outlaw gang was so unerring as to when the vehicle was, or was not, carrying gold shipments, that the city fathers finally summoned help from San Francisco. Aid came to Virginia City in the form of experts who had put down the era of violence and lawlessness in Northern California by organizing the Vigilance Committee, or Vigilantes . . . premature anathema to the Civil Liberties Union. A group of Vigilantes was formed in Virginia City.

Either their luck or their skill was monumental, for they came in with their quarry—none other than Sheriff Henry Plummer himself and most of his posse, including his principal deputy "Clubfoot George." Plummer, Clubfoot and several of the others were promptly hanged from the beams of their headquarters building. The others were hunted down, one by one, until twenty-four of the desperadoes had been dispatched, and somewhat peremptorily buried in the cemetery one block above and east of the gulch.

There Henry Plummer and his gang rested in peace for almost fifty years, until the historians, in their pursuit of accuracy and detail, enlivened the long-neglected community of Virginia City with a quarrel which sent the citizenry in search of old letters, newspapers, documents and brought old prospectors out of the hills by the score.

The Historical Society undertook to mark the graves of the bandits. It went well until the marker for Clubfoot George was about to be set in place. A grizzled old veteran stepped forward and told the historians that they had it all wrong . . . that Clubfoot was not in the grave which they had selected. That started it, and the contention raged for months.

Finally, it was agreed that there was only one thing

to do: exhume the skeletal remains of those in question, and to settle the matter.

The indelicate task was undertaken in the name of historical veracity, and the proof was uncontestable. One of the graves yielded a deformed and twisted human foot in an old blue Rockford sock semipetrified and joined to the bone.

George's foot, today, is on exhibit in the Virginia City Historical Museum.

It was while researching this fascinating episode of Montana's history that my class journeyed one day to Virginia City, where we were received cordially by an ancient judge of the county courts. We youngsters sat in his office, enthralled by his accounts of the gold-rush days along Alder Gulch.

The old judge said that at one period, a tong war broke out among the Chinese who had been imported by the thousands to shovel the soil and gravel of the gulch into the sluice boxes. According to his version of the tong battle, every round of ammunition in Virginia City was purchased and fired, but only one Chinese workman was killed and he died from a wound inflicted by a shovel. The old gentleman ruminated that on the basis of his observations in the intervening years, the story reflected not upon the marksmanship, but rather upon the charity and peacefulness, of the Chinese.

Personally, I was several years too late to participate in the exhuming of Clubfoot George. The assignments given my high-school class consisted of collecting and

submitting to the Historical Society other and somewhat more mundane information on the Vigilantes and
the habits, travels, interests and personalities of the
Plummer gang.

That was the climate of southern Montana. Every
town, every community had one or two old-timers still
living. While the adults gave them scant attention,
since they had heard it all before, young boys were
respectful audiences.

We in that little graduating class of Whitehall High
School, 1929, were the last of a unique generation. In
October, following that June commencement, the nation joined much of the world in the incalculable despair and bewilderment of the great depression. Since
then graduating classes have gone out to face one crisis
after another: three wars, cold wars, brush fires, and
nuclear "stare downs."

Were we, by some chance, the very last American
youngsters to be so free of anxieties and uncertain
prospects that we could enjoy being young?

Although the economic fortunes of our family were
modest and the railroads certainly did nothing to dis-
turb the "stabilization" of wages, I am sure the household budget might have provided me with an allow-
ance or pocket money. However, it never occurred to

me that there might be ways and means to finance my personal needs and desires other than earning and saving.

Consequently I experienced a meteoric career from washing windows, delivering groceries, cleaning out basements and splitting wood to initiating a newspaper route. At Big Timber, I ventured to place my order for twenty-five copies of the Sunday Minneapolis *Tribune*, complete with its heralded rotogravure section. It was something less than an assured profit-making venture, for I, in effect, had to purchase the paper at a wholesale price. It was not delivered to me on consignment. J. P. Morgan never enjoyed a greater sense of security and self-reliance than I on that first Saturday, when I sold out my twenty-five copies. Gradually, I increased the clientele to fifty.

My choice of the *Tribune* was not without some calculation. Minneapolis was rather the Scandinavian capital of the new world. It so happened that Big Timber boasted an exceptionally large Scandinavian population, and the Minneapolis Sunday *Tribune*, therefore, enjoyed a preconditioned market.

But my career as a newsboy was short-lived. I discovered that there was a much better market for my labor and my skills on the ranches of the community. Therefore, I turned the newspaper franchise over to a young friend and began to hire out as a ranch hand.

From the age of about fourteen to my final year in college, I spent most of the summers and many weekends on farms and ranches. In all modesty, I suspect I was rather proficient. I knew how to handle horses, and the tractor had not yet taken over. I was familiar with all the various pieces of farm and ranch equipment: the buck rake, bunch rake, the fork lift, the mower, binder, drill, harrow and baler. Invariably, I gave the employer a good return on his investment in me, for I was early in the field and late to leave it. The late-afternoon and early-evening hours always seemed the most profitable, for the horses had settled down to a steady pace and it was pleasant in the cool that invariably displaced the heat of midday. One of my early employers was a thrifty and taciturn Scotsman who had the reputation for demanding always a little over-time from his employees. I sent him clucking to himself the first day I worked on his ranch, when he had to shout at me from his front porch that it was time to bring in the horses and bed them down.

Ranch life and ranch work were satisfying. A day's labor was usually measurable. Where yesterday a field of alfalfa undulated in the wind, today it lay in a pattern of windrows, or the windrows disappeared one by one and the stacks took on dimension. The spring calves grew fatter and sleek as otters, and the bulls anticipated their July and August functions. On rainy days, when it was too wet to enter the fields, sagging gates were brought back to the horizontal, machinery repaired, fences tightened and harness mended. A shiny new board had taken the place of the splintered one which the horses had kicked out of the corral. The grain tank bulged with a new harvest of wheat, the gate swung easily on its new hinges, bales of hay lay in the field ready for stacking, the sickle bars had been sharpened, or the fencing wire was taut on its new posts. The chores never ceased, but somehow they were done.

In my third year of high school I worked in the Whitehall State Bank after classes and on Saturdays. My responsibilities were somewhat varied, ranging from the pedestrian tasks of sweeping out, dusting, filling inkwells and stoking the furnace, to posting the statements, sometimes posting the ledger as well, numbering checks and seeing to it that the outgoing mail got to the post office.

Mr. Roberts, the bank manager, graciously consented to my playing football that autumn and that necessitated a slight alteration of my schedule. I practiced with the team after classes, ate a hurried dinner at home and then went to the bank to discharge my responsibilities. Why Mr. Roberts put up with it, I was never certain, unless he felt it was his patriotic contribution to the excellence of the football team. If so, I hasten to add that Mr. Roberts' gift to the team was modest. My absence at right tackle would have left no gaping hole in the line.

One Thursday evening as I unlocked the front door of the bank and stepped inside, I was certain I heard a movement of some sort. I switched on the lights, looked into the toilet, the backrooms, and searched the basement. It was nothing. I finished my work and went home.

On Friday evening as I was posting the statements, I heard a slight scuffling and scraping which seemed to come from the ceiling. I concluded that something had evidently fallen onto the roof and was flapping about in the wind. I would go up there the following morning.

A slight skiff of snow fell that night and began to melt the next morning as the sun came up. However, as I opened the bank door, prepared to get the furnace going and to set up the establishment for a busy Saturday, I saw that water was trickling from the ceiling and forming a pool in the middle of the floor. I mopped up the puddle of water and then dragged a long ladder out of the basement, leaned it against the back of the building and climbed to the roof.

Near the skylight lay an old blanket. I picked it up and uncovered a yawning hole in the roof! Peering down into the dark attic, I saw the top of the vault, from which a generous number of the bricks had been removed and stacked to one side. As my eyes adjusted to the darkness I detected a tin can hanging from the electric wiring. Dropping through the opening in the roof, I found that the tin can contained a light bulb, which I turned in its socket. In the light, there at my feet was the whole story!

Drills, hammers, chisels, and tools of all description were laid out neatly on top of the vault. Where the bricks had been removed, the workman was down to the steel lining, and an acetylene torch had cut a gash of about eight inches.

I think my first bewildered reaction was one of utter disbelief mixed with a recollection of a sign which was hung prominently in the window of the bank: $40,000 REWARD FOR THE APPREHENSION OF ANYONE ATTEMPTING TO ROB THIS BANK. It also occurred to me that the project might be weeks old and that the bandit might have given up or had been frightened off and that the whole thing would end in just a tedious cleanup job.

I unscrewed the bulb, hoisted myself up through the hole in the roof, made certain that I left the blanket as I had found it, and returned to the bank.

But I had a genuine problem. Should I keep this electrifying information to myself, or did I have a solemn duty to report it to my employers?

The teller and assistant manager was a little gnome of a man, Mr. Hardin; but he was kind and gentle, almost repulsively neat and efficient, timid and grossly underpaid. Mr. Hardin had never been casual in his life; saying "Good morning" was a project to be well thought out and tidied up afterward.

Furiously, I debated with myself and realized that the longer I delayed the more I was inviting censure. Finally, I decided to take Mr. Hardin into my confidence.

Mr. Roberts was out of town that day, leaving Mr. Hardin in complete charge. When I told him what I had found on the roof, he began to flutter. To my disgust and consternation he went to the telephone to relay the information to the bank president, Mr. McKay, a white-haired and tight-fisted old Scotsman who had a rather substantial stake in virtually every enterprise in town. I could see that the whole adventure was about to be taken out of my hands and that I was going to be reduced to a most obscure role. Over the telephone, Mr. McKay said that he would summon the sheriff in Boulder, the county seat, and that we employees in the bank were to continue with our work as though nothing were amiss.

At noon, I slipped out and called my classmate and friend Bob Manlove, whose father was the town butcher. Bob agreed with me that he and I could play no important part in this impending drama, but he did propose that he would sneak his older brother's National Guard .45 pistol out of the house and he would come "armed" and join me after work.

Late that afternoon the sheriff and a deputy arrived from Boulder, and I was assigned to take them up to the roof of the bank building for an inspection. The two law-enforcement officers casually looked down through the hole in the roof and then began to discuss their strategy. They agreed that the chances of the bandit returning to his work that night—a Saturday night, when most of the stores were open to accommodate the ranchers—were very slight. No cautious robber, they reasoned, would venture to complete a job like this one on a Saturday night, but that he might undertake it the following night, on Sunday. Perhaps the project was an abortive one—abandoned for weeks. However, they did agree that a lookout should be posted, and that was my opportunity. I suggested that my friend Bob and I would hide behind the skylight and if the bandit appeared we could summon the sheriff and his deputy. The deputy wanted to know how I proposed getting off the roof of the building without alerting the robber. I had had the foresight to prepare for that. Bob and I could actually be on the roof of the adjoining building and yet be hidden behind the skylight. By walking across the roof of the adjoining building toward the alley, we could reach a telephone pole at the rear, climb down the convenient steel rungs and run to the hotel for the sheriff.

The two officers, candidly acknowledging no taste whatsoever for a cold night on a Whitehall rooftop, quickly agreed. Bob and I could hide behind the skylight. They airily told Mr. Hardin of the plans and retired to the hotel. Mr. Hardin went home, and the town settled down to a normal Saturday evening.

Bob and I choked down some food at my house. His brother's .45 was safely in a dresser drawer in my room. Mother inquired why we seemed to be in such a hurry, and we said we wanted to be sure to be on time for the movie that night. Safely out of the house with the .45 and a flashlight, Bob and I walked down to Main Street. We loitered for a while in front of the movie house and offered thin excuses to our friends why we were not quite ready to buy our tickets and go inside. Finally, we reasoned that we might as well see the movie because the robber, if he should appear that night, would probably arrive rather late and certainly we could hear him at work if we should arrive on the roof after he did. We went inside and enjoyed the picture—convinced, I believe, that the sheriff was quite correct: the bank robber, if he were to return at all, would certainly choose not to work on a Saturday night.

The movie came to an end, and Bob and I sauntered around the block, and approached the alley. On the corner, just inside the alley, Bob inserted a clip of ammunition in the .45, which had been bulging inside his shirt front all evening, pulled on the loading device, and a bullet slid noisily into the chamber. Cautiously we made our way down the dark alley to the telephone pole which was set where the bank and movie house joined. On up the alley were the drab backsides of J. C. Penney's, the grocery store and the drugstore on the corner. The far end of the alley was faintly lit by the small electric sign which hung over the side entrance of the hotel.

I recall having one spasm of misgiving as I gripped the cold steel rungs on the telephone pole and crept up toward the roof. Although I was protected by a heavy shirt and a warm jacket, it was going to be cold up there behind the skylight. I wished we had brought a blanket, but how would we have stolen it out of our homes without some serious questions?

As I raised my head above the level of the roof I paused to listen for a moment. No sound came from the bank building. In the dim light reflected from Main Street, I could see that the blanket over the hole in the roof was in place. Silently I lifted myself up, Bob behind me, and we edged to our post behind the skylight and crouched down.

Our vigil was brief. We had been in position no more than two or three minutes when I felt Bob's elbow in my side. On a telephone pole in back of the drugstore, at the far end of the alley, silhouetted against the light from the hotel sign, a figure loomed up. I could see the bill on his cap, a high collar turned up on a long heavy overcoat reaching well below the knees. Crouching, he made his way along the rear edges of the buildings, kicked the blanket away from the hole, stood and looked about for a long moment. Not more than twelve feet away, we lay terrorized behind the skylight. I could see him through the glass . . . ten feet tall . . . and mean! What in the name of all hell had I got myself into?

It seemed like hours before the figure somehow decided not to look behind the skylight, dropped down and disappeared through the hole. He took a long time adjusting both the blanket and his overcoat over the aperture he had cut in the roof. Presently, he went to work. The noise he made was unbelievable. He was a confident workman, assuming that anyone hearing his hammering and scraping would conclude it was coming from the garage or perhaps the railroad station across Main Street.

Bob nodded to me, and I edged toward the point of exit . . . the telephone pole. Once the roof creaked under my knee, and it sounded like an avalanche, but the noise of illicit industry from the cranny of the bank went on without interruption. As I crept down the pole my hands shook on the steel spikes. Safely on the ground, I sprinted up the alley, burst through the lobby of the hotel and shouted to the sleepy old clerk that I had to get to the sheriff. What was his room number? Infuriatingly, old Tom wanted to know what all the excitement was about and I had to placate him with a promise I would let him know right away, if he would only tell me where the sheriff was.

I raced down the upstairs hall and banged on the door. A sleepy voice from inside mumbled a response.

"He's there," I shouted. "He's in the bank!"

The weary, indifferent voice said, "Okay, okay. We'll be along." There followed the sounds of a body getting slowly and deliberately out of bed and fumbling about for a light switch.

I waited for a long moment and realized that the sheriff was going to take his time. He would probably then awaken the deputy and wait for him to get dressed. Bob, meanwhile, was alone on the roof.

I ran back down the stairs and past old Tom, who was peering out of the front door. As I sped down the alley and approached the bank building I realized that the pounding and scraping had ceased. Had he discovered something? What had happened to Bob? I dared not call out. I knew I had to climb back up that pole!

I peered over the top of the building. Bob was still there, the .45 clutched in his hand and aimed over the top of the skylight in the direction of the hole. But the silence was overwhelming. Not a sound came from the hole in the roof. Inch by inch I made my way to Bob.

"He's found out something," he whispered.

We lay there for a long time. I can recall how my pulse was banging in my ears.

Then the strain was somehow relieved by the obvious fact that something was going to happen . . . and quickly, as the overcoat and blanket over the hole began to move and then disappeared down into the chamber of horrors. Presently the bill on the cap and the high collar arose out of the opening, and then the shoulders of the man. My God! Could we let him get away? Would he come looking for us?

Bob made the decision. The .45 vomited a tongue of flame and shook the town. No artillery piece ever made that much noise.

Like a gopher the bandit ducked down in the hole, and the tragicomedy was galvanized.

Bob leaped from behind the skylight, shouting, "Come out of there! Put your hands up! Come out!"

Silence. Not a sound came out of the black cavern at our feet. I switched on the flashlight and beamed it into the hole and caught a glimpse of heavy boots and trouser legs.

"Come out of there!" we shouted.

Nothing happened.

Bob thrust the .45 into the hole, and again it roared and echoed over the sleepy little town.

A voice came out of the blackness—a defiant, angry voice. "I'm coming, goddamnit! Just stop that shootin!"

In the beam of the flashlight a stooped figure appeared beneath us, then straightened up until his head protruded out of the opening.

"Put your hands up," I yelled.

My flashlight was all over the place, on the bandit, in Bob's face, and on myself. Bob was waving the .45 about.

"Get your hands out of there," I demanded.

But he was fumbling about and no hands appeared.

In an outburst of hopeless desperation I shouted, "Get your hands up or I'll kick you right in the face!"

In the beam of the flashlight a strong rugged countenance looked up, and the bank robber replied with nerve-racking calm, "You kick me in the face, kid, and it'll be the last guy you kick in the face!"

He put his hands up through the hole!

Now what? We had brought nothing with which to tie up a prisoner. There was a momentary delay in further orders to our captive, and he waited patiently. But I had it! Furiously, I tore at my belt, unbuckled it and whipped it out of the trouser loops. Another moment of uncertainty developed. What to do with the flashlight while I tied his hands, and my trousers began to slide down over my hips. Bob was jumping about, still brandishing the enormous .45 and trying to prevent me from getting between him and the bandit.

At last rescue came! There were shouts, and the sheriff, the deputy, old Tom and a half dozen others came running across the rooftops. I was still holding the flashlight and belt in one hand and my trousers in the other. Quickly, the sheriff took charge. Bob was relieved of his .45, and the flashlight was snatched out of my hands. The robber was lifted out of the pit, and the entire entourage descended the telephone pole one by one. We marched up the alley, around the block, down Main Street, and burst into the pool hall.

The robber was in handcuffs by this time, and he sat quietly and confidently in a chair by one of the card tables. In response to the sheriff's questions, he said his name was Chester Casey, that his home was in Butte. Asked how long he had been working on the bank job, he said it had taken him longer than he had judged and that it "sure as hell" was not worth it. He volunteered the information that shortly after starting his "work" that night, he had detected that it had been discovered. He did not say how.

About that moment, Dad walked into the pool hall and saw me standing near the handcuffed prisoner. He demanded to know "what the devil" was going on, what was I doing there, and what was this all about? Graciously, the sheriff said I had captured a bank robber.

Dad had heard the cannonading of the .45 and was convinced that a gunfight had broken out in the pool hall.

Finally, someone thought to search the prisoner. A .38 was removed from the top of his boot!

Dad's shift at the depot had ended and we walked home. Both Bob and I were given rather stern lectures that night concerning the important distinction between heroism and plain damned foolishness. Dad vowed he was going to let the sheriff know what he thought about permitting two kids to maintain a lookout for a bank bandit. The whole affair was singularly lacking in heroics. The placid little farm and railroad town paid scant attention. I think we were denigrated by the somewhat universal conviction of the community that Casey the bankrobber was a bumbling idiot or he had simply spared a couple of brash kids.

Several weeks later, Bob and I were summoned out of class by an emissary from Mr. McKay. In a most generous manner we were told that since we were minors, Mr. McKay, in order to insure the payment of the $40,000 reward money, would make the application in his own name, and would we therefore sign the document which had been prepared? I believe the same paper, containing a most sketchy description of the capture, was submitted to our parents. In any event, a courteous note arrived ultimately from Mr. McKay and to it was attached a check for $50!

The years advanced . . . deliberately and in measured pace . . . as they have a way of doing in that period of childhood and youth when the rate of learning and remembering is so much greater than that of adulthood, and when time, therefore, is equally expanded. The twenties were an age . . . not a decade. We resided in no less than six communities between 1920 and 1927, and translated into experience, that meant new friendships to make, new towns to know, new rivers and mountains to explore. Out of the incomprehensible tangle of condensers, coils and gleaming tubes, the outside world began to assert itself, its voices borne into our lamplighted circle by the impulses from KGO, KFI, KOA, KDKA and the Henry Field Station.

These were the years of Teapot Dome and continued national debate over proposed legislation to outlaw child labor. The United States rejection of the World Court and the League of Nations prompted some second thoughts and mild controversy. President Warren G. Harding died in the Old Palace Hotel in San Francisco, and the Coolidge years began, characterized by an unstated and unwritten national temperament: "as little government as possible . . . and preferably less than that." To its tragic conclusion the nation followed the story of Floyd Collins and the agonizing day-by-day efforts to rescue him from the fastness of a Kentucky cave. In a classic confrontation of convictions and personalities, a clash between religious fundamentalism and agnosticism, William Jennings Bryan and Clarence Darrow argued the "Monkey Trial" in the stifling little courtoom in Dayton, Tennessee; and the exhausted Bryan, the "silver-tongued orator" from Nebraska, lay down to rest on his deathbed. With painted cheeks and knees, short skirts and shingled hair, the flapper destroyed forever the centuries of accumulated tradition concerning feminine attire. Americans danced the Charleston, and we began to hear of gangsters. A coal strike at Herrin, Illinois, claimed thirty-six lives; the Graf Zeppelin flew safely from Friedrichshafen, Germany, to Lakehurst, New Jersey; the Kellogg-

Briand Peace Pact, in a short-lived period of hope and confidence, was signed by sixty-two nations; Lindbergh flew the Atlantic; and I got my first pair of long pants! The acronym had barely made the dictionary. These were what writers and sociologists would call the Roaring Twenties.

With the singular exception of Butte, our Montana towns rode out the years in modesty and with no undue local disturbance beyond the occasional arrest of a bootlegger.

Marian, who many years later would be the organizer, chairman of the board, the matriarch of our family, became a dark-eyed little schoolgirl; and Peggy, our diminutive blond sprite, developed legs and marched off to first grade.

The majority of the teachers in the Whitehall primary and secondary schools boarded and roomed at the Palm Hotel or at a dormitory managed by the school board and located in what had been planned as the living quarters for the employees of the sugar factory. The sugar company had halted its construction about halfway through the project, leaving a tall smokestack, a row of executive houses and the dormitory. Frequently these "homeless" teachers were guests in our home for one of Mother's heralded dinners. Among these appreciative guests was Marian's teacher, Miss Samuelson.

Freshly out of teachers' college in North Dakota, Hedvig Samuelson was a singular girl: decidedly attractive, bright, and finely balanced between gay aggressiveness and reserved shyness. "Sammy" Samuelson was one of the very rare young teachers in that small community who managed the no mean feat of avoiding local gossip.

As I recall, it was during the second year of her tenure in the Whitehall school system that Sammy was taken ill with a severe attack of pneumonia. Aunt Cela, who was visiting us at the time, helped nurse her back to health, and she returned to the classroom for the spring months. On her doctor's advice, however, Sammy took a position for the following year in the primary school in Juneau, Alaska. From correspondence with some of the townspeople we then learned that she had contracted a mild case of tuberculosis and was going to spend some time in Phoenix, Arizona.

With what shock and dismay, about three years later, we saw Sammy's name and photograph on the front pages, frequently above lurid captions. From all over the nation friends sent the newspaper clippings. Sammy was a victim in the incredible Winnie Ruth Judd case, her dismembered body found in a trunk in the Los Angeles railroad station. A number of newspapers reprinted a bloodstained photograph taken from the trunk, and captioned it: HEDVIG SAMUELSON AND UNIDENTIFIED BOYFRIEND. It was a snapshot of Sammy and me standing on our front porch.

My first experience in "mass communication" came as the result of Dad's trade as a telegrapher. On the days of a World Series game, if it was Saturday or Sunday, Dad would write down the play-by-play reports as they came over the wire. A cluster of people would gather in the waiting room of the station, and I would bellow through the ticket window the play-by-play action of the game.

The same thing occurred the night of the great Dempsey-Firpo prize fight. I had the thrill of announcing the round-by-round action to a crowd of people gathered at the depot.

There was no logical explanation for the boisterous humor which characterized the vast majority of railroad men. The depots were often filled with roaring laughter as conductors, telegraphers, baggage men, engineers, brakemen, signalmen and section bosses gathered to swap stories and good-naturedly deprecate each other. Frequently, they would go to the most elaborate pains for the calculated development of a practical joke.

Dad was one of them . . . not as garrulous, blustering or bluff as many—Dad's humor was more waspish— but he held his own. It became a source of deep satisfaction to me over the years to note that the railroaders genuinely liked and respected Dad. "Pat" Huntley was the friend and companion of them all.

The engineers wore standard attire: the faded and freshly laundered denim bib overalls and jacket, the long-billed cap, the gauntlets with cuffs almost to the elbow, and the bandanna handkerchief always tucked fastidiously around the neck and under the jacket collar. This was the era when the steam locomotive reached its age of perfection, and the engineers were the great masters of their trade.

Jimmy Dean was an engineer on the North Coast Limited, and his fame had spread well beyond the division to the entire system, for he was the personification of Andy Gump. Jimmy's bristling mustache overpowered his chin to the degree that he seemed to be chinless.

"Ramblin' Jack" Wolverton for years was an engineer on 219 and 220, which ran between Butte and Billings, but previously he had held the run of "the Stub" . . . a small local train plying between Logan and Butte. How he had managed to stay out of trouble was a mystery.

Ramblin' Jack was not fastidious about the time schedule for the Stub. He frequently asked, "Who the hell cares whether that load of milk cans gets there on time?" Jack would remain beyond the deadline in his favorite haunt, the pool hall, across the street from the Logan yards. His firemen would begin blowing the whistle. Ultimately Jack would saunter out, casually inspect the wheels and undercarriage of his engine and climb aboard. He had been known to pull out of Logan thirty minutes late and arrive in Butte on time.

It was assumed that Ramblin' Jack, during the turn-around of several hours in Butte, would frequently visit one of the city's innumerable saloons, but no one ever proved it or made an issue out of it.

The Stub, on its return run to Logan, left Butte about ten o'clock at night, arriving in Logan around midnight. There was rarely a passenger on it. To enliven the run and produce some laughs, Jack and his firemen would occasionally hide in the cab of the engine and let the train roll down the last few miles of the Continental Divide, and streak through Pipestone, Whitehall and Cardwell. The locomotive was clearly out of gear . . . failing to slacken speed for the towns. Not a sound came from the great steam whistle.

The operator on duty had no choice. He would dash to the telegraph key and warn the points of the division to the east that the Stub was a runaway train—no fireman or engineer. In Livingston the dispatcher would check the division and prepare other trains to take sidings; the tracks would be cleared down the line.

Casually and with straight face, Jack and his firemen would roll sedately into Logan and solemnly profess ignorance of all the disturbance.

Or a sleepy telegraph operator would rouse himself as the Stub approached, and prepare to observe the engine cab, that he might make his report, or OS, to the dispatcher. Jack and his firemen would be in the tender, armed with chunks of coal, and let fly at the depot windows as the train hurtled past. The operator would dive under the telegraph bench and wait for the cascade of broken glass to subside.

To the dispatcher he would OS: "Train 222 out of Willow Creek eastbound on time."

Pete Ross was one of the "old heads," a great beaming Irishman with an inexhaustible supply of tales and jokes. Pete had hit a boulder one night, coming down the eastern side of the Continental Divide between Homestake and Pipestone. As the engine left the tracks and began to roll down the canyon side, the fireman leaped to safety. Pete, however, was on the wrong side of the cab and could not get out. He stayed with the engine while it rolled down the embankment. When the locomotive reached the bottom of the canyon and lay with its wheels in the air, Pete, not seriously hurt, began to clamber out, but a steam coupling had broken and the end of the pipe was embedded in the decomposed granite. As Pete made his exit from the wreck and thrashed about in the darkness, the steam pipe became a mighty sandblaster—emitting a spray of driven decomposed granite. The particles tore through his clothing like bullets and lodged in his flesh. For the rest of his life, Pete Ross was a unique shade of blue because of the thousands of small granite particles lodged in his body.

I shared a hospital ward with Pete once for about a week, and it was bedlam, featuring shortened sheets, exploding cigars, false love notes to the nurses, and general hilarity. Pete laboriously fashioned a large sign for the ward door: FRIEND OR ENEMA.

Jim Berry was an engineer on the "helpers"—the second engines which were attached to the trains at Butte and Whitehall for the laborious climb over the Continental Divide. Jim and his family lived in Whitehall.

One morning Jim was on the helper attached to train No. 41, the Burlington's passenger service to the West Coast, and which traveled on the Northern Pacific tracks from Billings to Seattle. The Burlington has long been a subsidiary of the Northern Pacific.

A few miles out of the Whitehall yards, 41 ran through an open switch, and Jim Berry's engine embedded itself in the ground, pinning him in the telescoped cab between the firebox and the tender. Jim died before they could extricate him.

A Whitehall schoolboy had broken the switch lock with a stone and thrown the switch.

On the fast expresses, engineers practiced and perfected their whistle styles, and frequently they would clamber over the great beasts in the shops and tinker with the whistle valves to alter the tone. Jimmy Dean could make the whistle of his engine moan and cry and wail, and the long final note would trail off imperceptibly into silence. As the North Coast Limited approached town, Jimmy's whistle sounded angry and ill-tempered, as though the cluster of buildings and the web of sidetracks were an intrusion. He bellowed his dislike for the town on the distant approach, snorted a warning where the highway crossed the tracks, shook up the community as he entered the block, gave the depot a blast as he shot by, and then the long wailing cry of remorse as he left the block and charged down the main line.

A local freight was standing at the depot one day, and a few boxes and bundles were being unloaded. A group of us boys were idling about, waiting for the train to pull out so we could cross the tracks. Suddenly the brakeman shouted at us, "Come here, you kids!"

He was standing in the door of the boxcar, holding about a dozen baseball bats. A carton had burst in the car, and baseball bats were rolling about.

"Come on," he urged. "Have a bat. Have two bats . . . three bats . . . bats for the whole damned town."

And with that he began throwing baseball bats out of the car and onto the platform.

On another occasion it seemed that a shipment of ink had been damaged. A brakeman tossed an ink-sogged carton at a freight handler, and that started it . . . a wild melee of ink-throwing and roars of laughter.

I saw Dad on the butt end of this sort of horseplay one day when he bent down to pick up something from the platform and a brakeman picked up a split sack of flour and dumped it over my father.

There was Tony, the section boss, a tremendous man, perhaps six feet five or six. Tony was of Polish descent. He had hired several of us youngsters one day to help him cut the weeds around the water tower and the toolhouse. We rode down to the end of the yards and to the water tower on the "speeder" (a small gasoline-driven vehicle with flanged wheels).

Out of nowhere a hailstorm developed, and suddenly we were being pelted with the biggest hailstones I have ever seen. They were about half the size of a baseball, and they hit with the force of a cannon shot. The only cover was the speeder. We youngsters had no difficulty scurrying under it, but Tony could not manage it. He got his head under the vehicle, but his great ample behind had to stay out and endure the punishment. Every time a hailstone would hit Tony on the bottom he would yell like a banshee and swear in Polish.

And there was "Potato Nose" Pete . . . a brakeman. Potato Nose was possibly the homeliest man I have ever known, with a nose which, indeed, was as large and bulbous as an Idaho potato. But he was a gentle man . . . always willing to hold up the switch engine for a few minutes to let us youngsters climb aboard a flatcar or gondola, and hook a ride through the yards.

And there were the traveling salesmen. The railroader harbored an acquired and intense dislike for the drummer. Too frequently this transient captain of commerce was much too ostentatious, too fast-talking, too urbane for the homely virtues of the railroader. Invariably, the salesman was conspicuously overdressed, usually to the point of the ridiculous. He did, indeed, wear loud checkered suits, silk shirts, screaming neckties—flashing darted socks and a skimmer. Half the time his shoes were turning to pale yellow from too much brown polish.

The hustling and indefatigable drummer never rode a passenger train from town to town if he could avoid it. Instead, he would make his deal with the brakeman or conductor of a freight train, and for a quarter or half dollar he would ride the caboose to his next stop. Such a situation inevitably led to a contest between train crew and salesman.

The freight train, of course, would discharge its cargo either on the main line or a siding from the box-cars toward the front or in the middle of the train. The caboose on which the salesman was to ride in some comfort was far down the tracks.

The salesman would take his position on the platform or at the side of the train, his skimmer secured, and his sample case well in hand. The cars began to roll by. While the salesman was contemplating the accumulating speed of the train and not looking, the brakeman was frantically signaling the engineer for more speed . . . to "pour on the coal." Faster and faster the cars rolled by as the caboose approached the station. The engineer had the throttle wide open, and the great locomotive was roaring its response.

Now the caboose and its handrails hurtled toward the uncertain drummer. He jammed his skimmer down on his head one last time, poised himself, ran alongside the caboose for a few steps with coattails flapping, threw his sample case at the caboose platform, and desperately lunged at the handrails!

He usually made it, but too often the train would glide away with the drummer's sample case on the caboose platform and the cursing salesman picking himself up from the cinders or off the station platform. His case was always faithfully left at the next depot up the line.

Those were the crowning years, too, of the hobo. I have not seen a traveler on a freight train since the Depression days. It is not only that our affluence has overwhelmed the hobo and drifter, but it is a sign that our country has been discovered. A large segment of our male population, I suppose, has seen the nation from the windows of troop trains. The rest have explored the regions in fast cars, or looked down on the magnificent topography from jet airplanes.

In the twenties, however, every freight train bore its human cargo. The hobo who was in a hurry rode the "blind baggage" (that small section just behind the tender and in front of the first express car). Some "rode the rods" . . . tying a cloth over their faces for protection against the flying cinders and stretching their bodies across the tie rods beneath the passenger coaches.

On the fringe of every Montana town was "the jungle"—the campsite of the bums and hobos. I spent many hours sitting around their fires, listening to their adventures, their tales of escape from overzealous "yard dicks" (railroad police). They had worked at every imaginable job in every imaginable town and city. Frequently, they were going to some promised job in a new locale, but more often they were vague about their future plans.

The jungle residents were of all ages and description. Rarely, however, they spoke with a foreign accent, indicating that they were not immigrants or first-generation Americans. There were old men with beards, and some were youngsters only a few years older than I. Universally the spirit of the jungle was one of surprising generosity. Food was shared, tobacco and cigarettes were passed around. Some were amazingly clean and tidy. The trees and bushes around the jungle were forever decorated with drying laundry. Basins, soap and razors were passed about, and an oil drum of hot water sat on a constant fire. Liquor was virtually unheard of in the hobo community, and the conversations were comparatively devoid of vulgarity.

These wanderers never spoke of homes or relatives, women or dear friends. Their talk was, for the most part, dedicated to former jobs, working conditions, climate, unscrupulous bosses and bargain eating-establishments in towns and cities and on the waterfronts of the nation. The storyteller and the man with the turn of phrase, the quipster and the comedian were greatly appreciated, and the campsites often rang with great howls of laughter. There were men who could recite poetry. Others sat and stared into the fire. The old and the infirm were patiently tolerated and even helped in a casual and indifferent way.

Never were we small boys chased out of a hobo jungle. Invariably we were given a matter-of-fact welcome. The men asked us the name of our town, how far it was to Butte or Billings, what the principal industries of the community were, and how cold it might get in winter. We were asked about school and whether we liked fishing and hunting. We were teased about girls. Often the men wanted to know if the sheriff or town constable ever arrested anyone who might wander into the community.

These were restless creatures. They did a good deal of wandering for the sake of wandering, and they were curious about all the areas of their native land. Many of them, perhaps, were malcontents, airing and sharing their grievances with each other. It may well be that organized labor is largely responsible for the vanished hobo, by its establishment of a machinery for the discharge of grievances.

On a number of occasions I recruited labor in the jungle camps. Mother was generous with the provisions of her bountiful kitchen, and the home-baked bread, the pies, cookies, preserves, hams, and meat loaves were excellent bargaining instruments when a particularly odious chore was to be done. The painting or whitewashing of a picket fence, for example, was sufficiently onerous that assistance was justified. I could usually find a helper in the hobo camp who would regale me with his adventures while we worked and who would take his pay in the form of a sack full of provisions from the kitchen.

But I was victimized a number of times. An earnest and articulate hobo would convince me that, indeed, he was on his way to a fine job in Seattle or St. Paul, that he had to grab the very next freight going that direction, but in return for a sack of lunch he would send me a dollar out of his very first pay check. With keen anticipation I handed over a number of splendid lunches, my name and address was carefully noted in a little book, but somehow the dollar remittances never arrived.

Up and down the long grades and through the mountain passes the freight trains moved the myriad products of farm and factory. At the close of the era of steam, the Northern Pacific boasted the greatest, most powerful and finest steam locomotive ever built: the V-5000 series, the 2-8-8-4 wheeled Yellowstone . . . one tremendous boiler over two tandem engines. From a two-thousand-foot altitude in the area around Miles City and Glendive, the Yellowstones waltzed the eighty-car trains, and longer, up the continental barrier to seven and eight thousand feet without undue whimper.

The efficiency of the great locomotive was demonstrated with a favorite stunt. The Northern Pacific would spot one of the incredible monsters on a town siding and invite a few of the well-known ladies of the community to come and gather at the head of the engine. Gloves would be passed out to the ladies, and they would be directed to push in unison against the cowcatcher . . . to push easily and gently. The ladies would oblige, and after a moment the great drive wheels would begin to turn on their ball bearings, and the women would push the gigantic monster along the track! The Yellowstone 2-8-8-4 was the culmination of the railroads' age of steam, the final and triumphant achievement of more than a hundred years of locomotive science.

Along the reaches of the Yellowstone, the Missouri and the Clark's Fork the great trains moved their cargoes. The long winding freighters, the cattle trains, the luxurious passenger units with reverberating names, the silk specials, the fruit expresses, the Shriner and American Legion charters labored through the Mullan, McDonald, Pipestone and Bozeman passes, shot through the placid little towns, and raced up and down the long valleys.

Epilogue

The tale is told. I apologize for its failure to come to some shattering and monumental climax . . . for the way it must end in a sigh. Its lesson is obscure; its message is modest. I am still not certain that these recollections should have been other than quiet and private memories, but I was pitted against the beguiling flatteries of a wife who is given to a case of hero worship, and I otherwise succumbed to the generous urgings of well-meaning friends.

But this is the way it was that fortune and the undaunted aspirations of parents and the restless searchings of grandparents permitted me to know and remember a few years and a few scenes of the nation's last frontier.

I have seen the sunlight dancing off the Spanish Peaks or the solemn volcanic head of Old Hollowtop.

I have heard the harmony of a meadowlark song

hanging like jewels on the morning sunshine and promising, "It's a lovely day!"

I have seen the nighthawks at dusk, mysterious white dots gleaming on their underwing, or curlews running awkwardly across the grassland, feigning injury, to decoy the interloper away from the nest.

I have heard the music in the recitative of the counties . . . the majestic names with rolls of mountain thunder: Choteau, Glacier, Cascade, Teton, Silver Bow, Musselshell, Big Horn, Wibaux and Deer Lodge; or the soprano names of Sweetgrass, Stillwater, Golden Valley, Rosebud, Wheatland and Judith Basin.

I have seen Doc Minnick, bundled and heavy-coated to shapeless figure, hunched forward in the seat of the buckboard, his horse plodding up the hill from the flats past the dreary little cemetery where Grandma lies. Wisps of snow are picked up by the iron tires of the rig and dissolved by the trenchant wind.

I have learned the tune of the towns: Kalispell, Cut Bank, Anaconda, Helena, Missoula, Big Timber, Glendive, Armington, Sun River, Sandcoulee, Shawmut, Black Eagle, Willow Creek, Three Forks, Red Lodge, Fishtail, Ryegate, Roundup, Circle, Spotted Robe, Sunburst, Big Arm, Wolf Creek, and the grace-note name of Twodot.

This time of year, the wheat fields of the high plains and the foothills of the Beartooth and Absaroka ranges, up above the involuted windings of the Rosebud and the Little Bighorn, are golden seas.

I have stood on the station platform at Whitehall on frost-touched October mornings to watch No. 220, with Pete Ross in the cab, slip cautiously down the eastern face of the Continental Divide and send the compounded echoes flying down the valley with a long soulful whistle for Pipestone crossing.

I have listened to the angry 2-8-8-4 Yellowstone's quarreling with the grade on Bozeman Pass, emitting great dinosaurian coughs and snorts, then falling instantly silent in the long black void of Muir Tunnel.

On the slopes of the foothills and in the bottom land along the Yellowstone, from Billings to Livingston and on upriver, I have seen the sleek Herefords staring bemusedly across the valley, forelegs retracted up under their briskets.

I have "played my cards right" and prevailed upon old Chief Two-Gun White-Calf, his proud profile memorialized on the buffalo nickel, to pose with me for a picture outside his lodge.

I have captured the feel of things . . . the high, wide and handsome past . . . with a stroll up Last Chance Gulch, where the gold in a basement excavation will still yield almost enough for the cost of the first story. I have turned to the left at the end of the Gulch and climbed the hill to walk past the great old mansions, domed and cupolaed and many-gabled, crenelated and gingerbreaded, relics of the gold-boom years, when Helena's imports of champagne, caviar, silken finery and Spanish lace rivaled those of New York.

I have seen the "big stack" of Anaconda's smelter painted against the unbounded dome of sky.

From the rimrocks I have looked down upon the rooftops of Billings: tree-shaded, neat and tidy.

Chet Huntley

I have fished the Yellowstone, the Rosebud, Little Rosebud, the Stillwater and Bridger Creek; and in late autumn I have worked the swift water of the Madison below McCallister Lake when the Lochlaven were in spawn. They were brown and red-spotted flashes of fury as they hit a Lake Clear Wobbler or a Devon minnow, not to feed but to protect their spawn.

I have watched the squadrons of Canadian honkers, snow geese, teel and mallards pursuing their primordial flight paths, and I have listened to dark nights filled with their honking and calling.

By saddle and pack horse I have climbed to the lofty mountain passes and lush meadows of the Bitteroot Range to sleep under blazing stars and beside a gushing snow-fed stream. I have been admonished into reverent silence by the mysteries of the great conifer forests and felt like an intruder. The forests are the exclusive property of the soughing wind, its furred and feathered denizens, shafts of sunlight, and caverns of shadow. The lodgepole pine, straight as a plumb line, engage the blue-black and hulking Engleman spruce in competition for the sky. The lady of the forest is the Douglas fir . . . soft and more demure; refusing to grow at all if she cannot do it properly . . . harmoniously limbed and perfectly contoured. The white pine and cedar stay off by themselves, spurning the mutual protectiveness of the forest, braving it out on the crags and buttes and challenging the elements. On the fringes of the meadows, like choruses of little virgins, the aspen giggle and quiver in nervous ecstacy.

Across the pastures and open range land, I have seen

Danny and Elena; Roy and Ivy and Carrie; Helen, Steve and Rudy trudging to school.

I have seen Wolf Creek on a springtime morning.

Grandpa is not too long in his grave at Casper, Wyoming, but I have seen him on the brow of the hill, tall and straight, him and horse embossed against the sky, waving his hat in welcome as we drove up the lane. And I have seen him standing in the wagon bed, working the confusion of lines, urging Rex and Savage, exhorting Bill and Brownie, coaxing Polly and Prince, and threatening Chub and Charlie across the ford on the river.

I have heard the forlorn and eerie howl of the coyotes ululating on the wind.

I have seen the storms howl down from the Arctic North, seizing the land in blinding furies of snow, ice, wind and frightful cold. The storm is invariably followed by a long period of silence . . . a time lapse for nature to dissolve her angry countenance. The land lies rigid, punished, hesitant to move lest it splinter. Then the clouds let the light through, a chinook whispers passionately at the snow, the sun blazes upon the white world, and all is forgiven.

I have seen Pat Huntley pounding the key at Big Timber and handing orders to an extra to take siding at Greycliff for the North Coast Limited westbound.

The scent of hay is sweet on the Saco flats, and the cars no longer wallow in the gumbo streets of the town. Cement sidewalks have taken the place of the old boardwalks which once undulated along the line of storefronts.

The ghostly shafts and lateral drifts of the Mountain Con, the Badger, the Emma and the rest are exposed on the walls of the pit as the giant shovels bite and claw into "the richest hill on earth," and the trucks cart it away to the smelter. The miners and muckers are now teamsters. The open pit has displaced Walker's, Mudro's Grill, the 123 Club, Mercury Street and the Rocky Mountain Café. Jerry Murphy no longer directs traffic and the interests of the city from his sentinel post at Park and Montana.

Traffic on the Northern Pacific is controlled by automatic signal system. The little depots are closed . . . sold off to farmers and ranchers for sheds or barns. The telegraphers are all but gone.

There are no more mudholes on the Yellowstone Trail. It bears the name "U. S. Highway #10" as it swings and curves majestically through the valleys and over the mountain passes.

Ranchers, in their own Cessnas, fly to the Hereford Show in Denver.

But I have seen the buffalo grass . . . rolling, rolling on its West Bench ocean . . . and singing its assonant song to the wind.

ABOUT THE AUTHOR:

CHET HUNTLEY was born in Cardwell, Montana, and grew up on a northern Montana ranch, in the little town of Saco, and a succession of other towns in the southern part of that state. He attended Montana State College at Bozeman, the Cornish School of Arts in Seattle, and received his B.A. from the University of Washington at Seattle. He was a news broadcaster and commentator for radio stations in Seattle, Spokane, Portland and Los Angeles, and has been with NBC in New York since 1955.